How to Use This Book

Look for these special features in this book:

SIDEBARS, **CHARTS**, GRAPHS, and original **MAPS** expand your understanding of what's being discussed—and also make useful sources for classroom reports.

FAQs answer common **F**requently **A**sked **Q**uestions about people, places, and things.

WOW FACTORS offer "Who knew?" facts to keep you thinking.

TRAVEL GUIDE gives you tips on exploring the state—either in person or right from your chair!

PROJECT ROOM provides fun ideas for school assignments and incredible research projects. Plus, there's a guide to primary sources—what they are and how to cite them.

Please note: All statistics are as up-to-date as possible at the time of publication.

Consultants: C. Scott Brockman, Senior Geologist, Retired, Ohio Geological Survey;
William Loren Katz; Warren Van Tine, Professor of History, The Ohio State University

Book production by The Design Lab

Library of Congress Cataloging-in-Publication Data
Stille, Darlene R.
 Ohio / by Darlene Stille.
    p. cm.—(America the beautiful. Third series)
 Includes bibliographical references and index.
 ISBN-13: 978-0-531-18579-7
 ISBN-10: 0-531-18579-6
 1. Ohio—Juvenile literature. I. Title.
F491.3.S74 2008
977.1—dc22   2007037177

AMERICA ★ THE ★ BEAUTIFUL

Ohio

BY DARLENE R. STILLE

Third Series

Children's Press®
An Imprint of Scholastic Inc.
New York ★ Toronto ★ London ★ Auckland ★ Sydney
Mexico City ★ New Delhi ★ Hong Kong
Danbury, Connecticut

CONTENTS

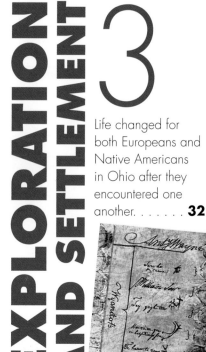

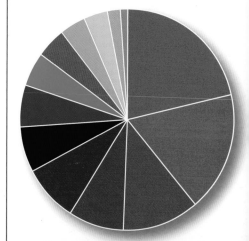

4
GROWTH AND CHANGE

Land companies laid out the first cities, railroads were built, and Ohioans fought for rights. . . **42**

5
MORE MODERN TIMES

Ohio's people and industries survived the Great Depression, and supported U.S. efforts in two world wars. . . . **58**

9
TRAVEL GUIDE

Visit "popcorn heaven," fly down a roller coaster, check out a lighthouse, or soak up history at a president's home. **108**

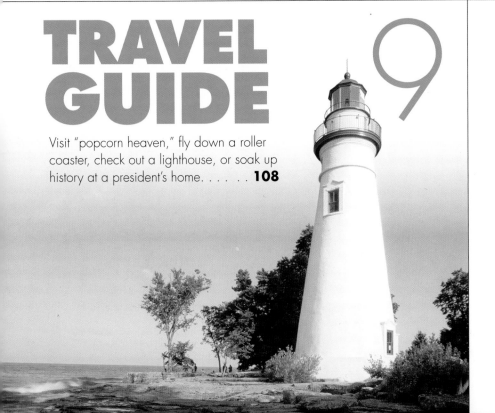

PROJECT ROOM

★

CANADA

MICHIGAN

LAKE ERIE

Marblehead
Lighthouse

TOLEDO

PENNSYLVANIA

Rock and Roll
Hall of Fame

Maumee

SANDUSKY

CLEVELAND

Cuyahoga

American Civil War
Museum of Ohio

African Safari
Wildlife Park

Sandusky

Cedar Point
Amusement Park

YOUNGSTOWN

Edison Birthplace
Museum

AKRON

Neil Armstrong
Air & Space Museum

CANTON

Pro Football
Hall of Fame

INDIANA

Scioto

OHIO

Schoenbrunn Village
State Memorial

Appalachian Plateau

Wyandot Popcorn
Museum

Muskingum

Ohio

SunWatch Indian Village/
Archaeological Park

DAYTON

Ohio Statehouse

Great Miami

The Horseshoe,
Ohio State University

COLUMBUS

Scioto

Hocking Hills
State Park

WEST VIRGINIA

Cincinnati Zoo &
Botanical Garden

CINCINNATI

Ohio

KENTUCKY

N
W   E
S

0   30
Miles

QUICK FACTS

State capital: Columbus
Largest city: Columbus
Total area: 44,825 square miles
(116,096 sq km)
Highest point: Campbell Hill, 1,550 feet
(472 m), located in Logan County
Lowest point: Ohio River, 455 feet
(139 m), located in Hamilton County

NEW YORK

PENNSYLVANIA

N.J.

DELAWA

MARYLAND

VIRGINIA

Welcome to Ohio!

HOW DID OHIO GET ITS NAME?

In the summer of 1669, a group of French explorers set off in bark canoes, paddling down the St. Lawrence River from Canada. Iroquois people had told them of a big river deep in the wild country south of Lake Erie. Finding the river was worth a dangerous journey. It might carry them to China, where they could trade for valuable silks and spices. Did the Iroquois mean the Ohio River or the Mississippi River? Historians are not sure. The Iroquois called the river "O-Y-O," which means "great river." The land west of the Appalachian Mountains and north of the Ohio River was, for a time, called the Ohio country. When Ohio became a state, the name stuck.

OHIO

8

READ ABOUT

Brandywine Falls in the Cuyahoga Valley National Park, which lies along the Cuyahoga River

CHAPTER ONE

LAND

★

THERE ARE MORE THAN 44,000 MILES (70,800 KILOMETERS) OF RUSHING RIVERS AND GENTLE STREAMS CUTTING THROUGH OHIO. Most flow into one mighty river—the Ohio River in the south. The Cuyahoga, Maumee, and Sandusky rivers flow into Lake Erie in the north. The state's lowest point is along the Ohio River, 455 feet (139 meters) above sea level. The highest point is Campbell Hill in Hamilton County at 1,550 feet (472 m) above sea level.

These grooves in Ohio limestone were carved by a glacier some 35,000 years ago.

Q8 DID DINOSAURS LIVE IN OHIO?

A8 They probably did, but no one has ever found a dinosaur fossil in Ohio. Ohio has no rocks dating from between 245 million and 65 million years ago, when dinosaurs roamed the earth. Why? Perhaps Ohio was above sea level then and there was no sediment to cover the dinosaur bones. Or, perhaps fossils did form, but wind and water eroded all traces of them.

OHIO'S PREHISTORIC PAST

Why do some parts of Ohio have plains or rolling hills and other parts have rugged cliffs and deep valleys? Why is some Ohio soil rich and good for growing crops whereas other soil is poor? Where did the fossil fuels coal, oil, and natural gas in eastern Ohio come from?

The answers to some of these questions have to do with glaciers, enormous rivers of ice as much as 1 mile (1.6 km) thick. Moving like giant icy paws, the glaciers crept down into Ohio from Canada. Beginning about 1.6 million years ago, the glaciers advanced four times and then retreated north again. As they moved, they dragged along stones as big as boulders and as small as pebbles. These stones changed the shape of the land. The last glacier retreated back into Canada about 10,000 years ago, leaving behind the landscape that shapes Ohio today.

In two-thirds of Ohio, the glaciers flattened hills and ground up rocks to start forming plains with rich soil. The last glacier dug out what became Lake Erie. The glaciers never reached southeastern Ohio. Hundreds of millions of years ago, that area was a warm, wet swamp. Swamp plants died and built up into thick layers under the water. Over time, layers of sand, silt, and other **sediment** built up over the dead plants. The weight of the sediments over time turned the dead plants into a sodlike substance called peat. Over millions of years, as the peat sank deeper into the earth, high pressure and temperatures hardened it into coal. Oil, natural gas, and other fossil fuels also formed from ancient plant materials.

WORD TO KNOW

sediment *material eroded from rocks and deposited elsewhere by wind, water, or glaciers*

Ohio Geo-Facts

Along with the state's geographical highlights, this chart ranks Ohio's land, water, and total area compared to all other states.

Total area; rank . . . . . . 44,825 square miles (116,096 sq km); 34th
Land; rank . . . . 40,948 square miles (106,055 sq km); 35th
Water; rank . . . . 3,877 square miles (10,041 sq km); 14th
Inland water; rank . . . . 378 square miles (979 sq km); 37th
Great Lakes; rank . . . . 3,499 square miles (9,062 sq km); 4th
Geographic center . . . . Delaware County, 25 miles (40 km)
north-northeast of Columbus
Latitude . . . . 38° 27' N to 41° 58' N
Longitude . . . . 80° 32' W to 84° 49' W
Highest point . . . . Campbell Hill, 1,550 feet (472 m),
located in Logan County
Lowest point . . . . Ohio River, 455 feet (139 m),
located in Hamilton County
Largest city . . . . Columbus
Longest river . . . . Ohio River, 451 miles (726 km)

Source: U.S. Census Bureau

 **Ohio could fit inside Alaska, the largest state, 14 times.**

Ohio Topography

Use the color-coded elevation chart to see on the map Ohio's high points (orange to yellow) and low points (green to dark green). Elevation is measured as the distance above or below sea level.

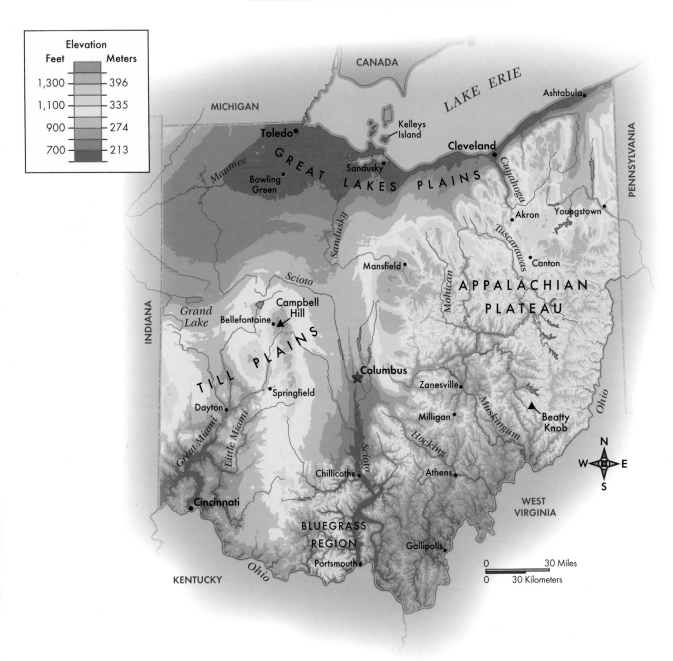

LAND REGIONS

Flat plains and rolling hills make up the landscape of northwestern and central Ohio. This part of the state was once covered with buckeye trees, making the Buckeye State an appropriate nickname for Ohio. Pioneer settlers cut down the buckeyes to build log cabins. Now the rich soil is plowed into fields that produce corn, soybeans, and other crops.

Southeastern Ohio is different. Its rugged cliffs and valleys have poor soil. But the area has mineral riches in the forms of coal, oil, and natural gas. Such natural resources helped Ohio become a major industrial state.

Geologists divide the state into four regions: the Great Lakes Plains, the Till Plains, the Appalachian Plateau, and the Bluegrass Region.

Great Lakes Plains

The Great Lakes Plains are along the shores of Lake Erie. In eastern Ohio, the strip is about 5 miles (8 km) across, widening to more than 50 miles (80 km) near Toledo. The Great Lakes Plains, formed from an ancient lake bottom, are flat and low, except for sand dunes along the lakeshore. The northwestern Great Lakes Plains was once a muddy area called the Great Black Swamp. Pioneer farmers drained the swamp and turned it into Ohio's richest farmland.

Till Plains

The Till Plains is a region of rich soil and rolling hills south of the Lake Plains in western Ohio. Glaciers deposited rock and soil to form these hills. The Till Plains contain both the highest and lowest points in Ohio.

A great white heron takes flight at the Ottawa National Wildlife Refuge on Lake Erie near Toledo.

Appalachian Plateau

The Appalachian Plateau makes up the eastern part of Ohio. The plateau is a flat area that is higher than the land to the west. Geologists further divide the Appalachian Plateau into glaciated areas, which were once covered with glaciers, and unglaciated areas, which were never covered with glaciers. The unglaciated areas contain gorges, cliffs, and waterfalls formed by winding streams. Forests line the steep hills.

The glaciated Appalachian Plateau is much less rugged. The glaciers ground down rough terrain, smoothed out hills and ridges, carved out small lakes, and created wet bogs.

Bluegrass Region

The Bluegrass Region is the smallest natural land area in Ohio. It is part of the larger Bluegrass Region in neighboring Kentucky to the south. The name of this area comes from a type of grass that is good for lawns and pastureland. Small, flat-topped hills cover most of the Bluegrass Region.

SEE IT HERE!

HOCKING HILLS STATE PARK

There are plenty of rock shelters to explore in Hocking Hills State Park near Logan. The shelters are carved out of sandstone, a soft rock that was laid down in layers 350 million years ago when this part of Ohio lay beneath a warm, shallow sea. The shelters formed when streams eroded the rock.

WEATHER AND CLIMATE

Long, warm summer days are great for fishing or swimming in Ohio's many lakes and streams. Summer temperatures in Ohio sometimes soar above 100 degrees Fahrenheit (38 degrees Celsius). But cold winds blow across the state in the wintertime, when temperatures can plunge to –10°F (–23°C). Southern Ohio has the warmest summer temperatures and the mildest winters.

Cold, dry air flows down from Canada, and warm, moist air pushes up from the Gulf of Mexico. The two air masses often clash over Ohio, creating storms. Southern Ohio gets the most precipitation. Cincinnati is the wettest city in the state, averaging 42.6 inches (108 centimeters) a year in rain and snowfall. Snow can fall anywhere in Ohio, but the northwestern part of the state gets the most. Cleveland has recorded more than 100 inches (254 cm) of snow in winter.

Weather Report

This chart shows record temperatures (high and low) for the state, as well as average temperatures (July and January) and average annual precipitation.

Record high temperature . . . . 113°F (45°C) near
Gallipolis on July 21, 1934
Record low temperature . . . . –39°F (–39°C)
at Milligan on February 10, 1899
Average July temperature . . . . .75°F (24°C)
Average January temperature . . . . .28°F (–2°C)
Average yearly precipitation . . . . 38 inches (97 cm)

Source: National Climatic Data Center, NESDIS, NOAA, U.S. Department of Commerce

A flooded street in Cincinnati, January 1937

EXTREME WEATHER

Ohio has its share of news-making weather events, such as tornadoes. These rapidly twisting, violent winds often rip through the plains of western Ohio. One of Ohio's worst tornadoes roared through Xenia on August 3, 1974. The winds leveled 300 homes and damaged almost half the town. Between Xenia and Wilberforce, 32 people were killed and about 1,300 were injured. A record 28 tornadoes touched down in Ohio on July 12, 1992, the most ever in a single day.

Winter snows are great for winter sports, such as skiing in northeastern Ohio. Sometimes, however, the state gets too much of a good thing. Blizzards are a wintertime hazard in Ohio. The snow can become so thick that it causes a whiteout, with zero visibility. During the blizzard of January 1978, two days of heavy snow followed by blasting winds shut down most of the state.

THE FLOOD OF 1937

In addition to being a place for boating and fishing, the Ohio River is a highway for commerce. Barges carry farm products and manufactured goods along the river. Cities, towns, and farms along the river's banks, however, live with a constant threat—flooding. One of the state's greatest disasters was the Ohio River flood of 1937. Beginning on January 13, record-breaking rains pounded the state for a week and a half. Water flowed from the soggy ground into the Ohio River, and the river began to rise. At Cincinnati, the river crested at 80 feet (24 m) above the normal flood stage. The downtown was almost submerged under water. Incredibly, only 10 people died. Since then, steps have been taken to control the river water. But floods can still occur. In fact, a major flood took place along the river in 1997.

Purple coneflowers and black-eyed Susans cover an Ohio roadside.

PLANT LIFE

Before European settlers arrived, Ohio was 95 percent hardwood forest. The most common trees in the ancient forests were beeches, tulip trees, sweet buckeyes, and sugar maples. Today, the most common trees are beeches, black walnuts, hickories, maples, sycamores, oaks, white ashes, white elms, and poplars. Ohio also has many species of wildflowers, including black-eyed Susans, wild violets, blazing stars, coneflowers, trilliums, and lady's slippers. The scarlet carnation, which is not wild, was chosen as the state flower in 1904 in memory of slain president William McKinley, who was from Ohio.

Ohio National Park Areas

This map shows some of Ohio's national parks, monuments, preserves, and other areas protected by the National Park Service.

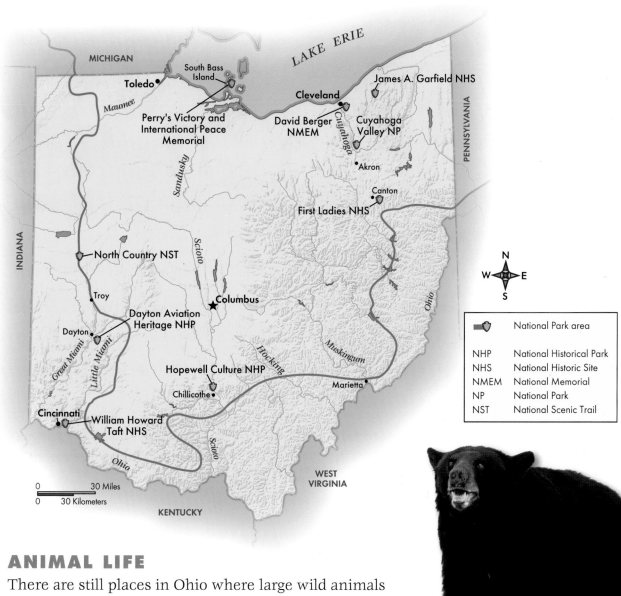

	National Park area
NHP	National Historical Park
NHS	National Historic Site
NMEM	National Memorial
NP	National Park
NST	National Scenic Trail

ANIMAL LIFE

There are still places in Ohio where large wild animals live. White-tailed deer thrive in forests and in wooded areas along farm fields. A few black bears and bobcats have been spotted in remote eastern forests. Many

Black bear

ENDANGERED SPECIES

Early Ohio settlers cut down forests that were home to black bears and bobcats, and later settlers cleared more land for farms and cities. In the 20th century, commercial developers turned fields and forests into factories and shopping malls. Many large wild animals, birds, and plants in Ohio became endangered because their habitats were destroyed. Thanks to efforts aimed at protecting black bears, the number of these animals is now on the rise in remote eastern forests. Other endangered species in Ohio include the snowshoe hare, the sandhill crane, the osprey, and the peregrine falcon. The Lake Erie water snake and the bald eagle are two threatened species.

Snowshoe hare

A flock of Canada geese takes flight from the frozen Brady Lake.

small animals, such as squirrels, woodchucks, opossums, raccoons, skunks, and even red foxes, scamper through fields and backyards.

Bird-watchers have spotted about 275 species of birds in Ohio, including blackbirds, woodpeckers, thrashers, cardinals, chickadees, pheasants, and wild turkeys. Ducks and geese paddle around on lakes and streams. Red-tailed hawks can be seen soaring through the sky. Ohio's lakes and streams are home to more than 160 species of fish, including bluegills, bass, perch, sturgeons, and walleyes.

HUMANS AND THE ENVIRONMENT

Since the first settlers arrived, humans have continued to change Ohio's environment. They mined coal that was used to fuel factories and power plants. But burning coal produced waste that polluted the air and water. To clean up existing environmental problems and prevent new ones, the Ohio legislature passed laws limiting the amount of waste that industry can dump into the air and water. The state government is also restoring some of its forests. In 1940, only 12 percent of Ohio was forest. Now forested areas cover more than 20 percent of the state.

In the late 1800s, the Ohio shore of Lake Erie became one of the great American manufacturing centers. It also became one of the country's most polluted regions. Chemical waste from factories and fertilizers from farmlands poured into the lake. The pollution killed fish and other wildlife. In the 1960s, environmentalists declared Lake Erie "dead." Ohio worked with the governments of Canada and the United States to control pollutants entering the lake. By the late 1990s, many fish were once more swimming in the lake. Today, people again enjoy the beaches along the shores of Lake Erie, but the lake and its inhabitants are still not out of danger.

M. SIOBHAN FENNESSY: OHIO ENVIRONMENTALIST

Most people are in favor of saving endangered animals such as the bald eagle and the cheetah. But who cares about liverworts—small rootless and flowerless plants that grow in wet areas? M. Siobhan Fennessy does. Ohio has lost about 90 percent of its wetlands, and this Columbus native has made preserving and restoring them her life's work. She has worked with Ohio's Environmental Protection Agency, researching wetlands and applying what she learns to help restore those that have been damaged or lost. She is currently an associate professor of Biology and Environmental Studies at Kenyon College.

 Want to know more? See www.kenyon. edu/x21042.xml

ALIEN INVADERS

In the late 1980s, a species called the zebra mussel invaded Lake Erie. Zebra mussels are native to eastern Europe and western Asia. They were brought to the lake unintentionally on ships that had sailed around the world. Zebra mussels have become a huge problem in Lake Erie and the other Great Lakes. They clog water intake pipes, boat engines, and the screens at water treatment plants. They also devour massive amounts of plankton—tiny plants and animals that float in the water—leaving little for fish and native mussels to eat. By the early 2000s, the water of Lake Erie looked clear because the zebra mussels had eaten so much of the plankton that is vital to the lake's food chain.

READ ABOUT

Early hunters using stones and spears to kill a mammoth

Adena tablet

c. 10,000 BCE

People arrive in what is now Ohio

c. 2300 BCE

Native people in Ohio begin to plant seeds

▲ c. 800 BCE

The Adena culture appears

CHAPTER TWO

FIRST PEOPLE

★

AS THE LAST GLACIERS RETREATED TO CANADA ABOUT 10,000 YEARS AGO, PLANTS AND ANIMALS APPEARED ALONG THEIR ICY EDGES. Pine, spruce, and fir trees began to grow. Then came the strange animals to eat the plants. Imagine a giant beaver more than 8 feet (2.4 m) long or a giant ground sloth as big as an elephant! Other enormous mammals, such as mastodons and woolly mammoths, were also present.

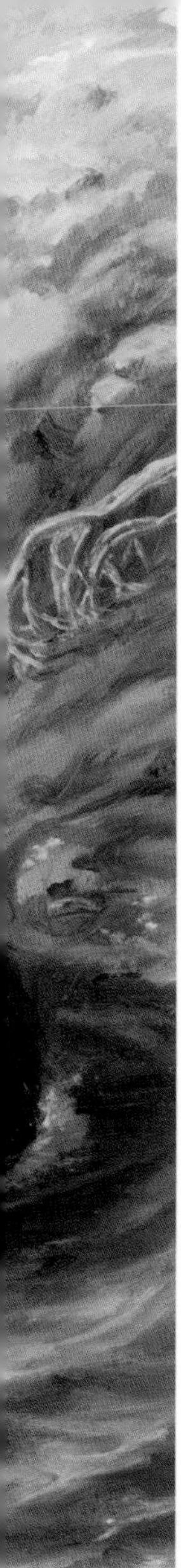

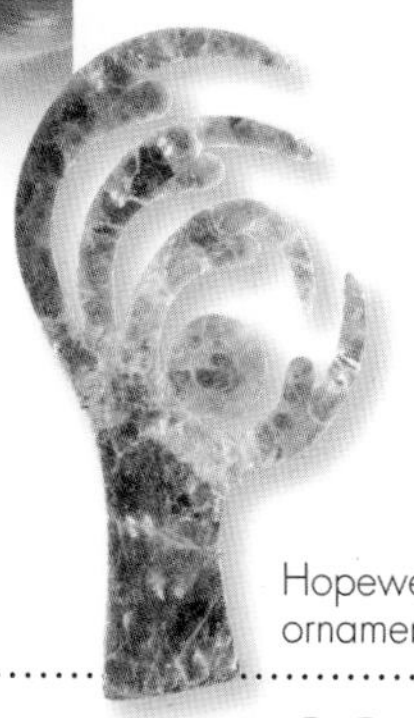

Hopewell
ornament

▲ **c. 100** BCE
*The Hopewell culture
appears*

c. 1000 CE
*The Fort Ancient
culture is established*

1600–1700
*New Native American
groups move into Ohio*

THE FIRST PEOPLE

At least 13,000 years ago, people began to arrive in North America. Scientists think they followed the wild animals from Asia by walking over a land bridge to Alaska when the sea level was much lower. Over time, some of the descendants of these people made their way to the area we know as Ohio. **Archaeologists** call them Paleo-Indians. They lived in small groups of 30 to 40, moving constantly as they hunted game and gathered nuts and berries. At first, they hunted with wooden spears. They used rocks to chip pieces of flint into sharp, deadly points for their spears. Archaeologists dig up these prehistoric spear points and study them for clues about how the early people lived, but they know very little about the first Ohioans. These people probably wore animal skins. They may have lived part of the year in rock shelters.

As the glaciers retreated, the ice age ended in Ohio. The climate grew warmer, and the huge mammals became extinct. Early people adapted by hunting smaller animals and fishing. Over time, they learned to make axes and other tools.

They moved often in search of food and lived in portable homes made of wooden poles covered with bark or animal skins. As generations passed, the number of people and hunting bands in the region grew. They moved around in smaller and smaller areas as there was less available territory for each group. Around 2300 BCE, some groups began to settle in more permanent villages and plant seeds instead of searching for wild plants.

EARLY FARMERS

Ohio's first farmers appeared around 800 BCE. They left behind mysterious mounds of piled-up dirt.

WORD TO KNOW

archaeologists *people who study the remains of past human societies*

FAQ

Q8 WHERE DID OHIO'S FIRST PEOPLE GET FLINT FOR ARROWHEADS?

A8 Early people found an 8-mile-long (13 km) deposit of this hard rock in east-central Ohio. They dug pits and chipped out pieces of flint. This place, now called Flint Ridge, is protected as a state memorial.

Flint arrowhead

This painting shows ancient Adena people gathering at a ceremonial site in the Hocking River valley.

Archaeologists named the culture Adena, after a site where some mounds were found.

The Adena people planted crops such as sunflowers, squash, and pumpkins. Because they planted food crops, they did not have to move around constantly. The Adena culture developed new skills to match their new way of life. They learned to mold clay into pottery. They made clay pots for cooking and storing food. They also carved pipes and figures out of stone.

When they died, some Adenas, possibly the leaders, were buried in wooden coffins. The Adena people built cone-shaped mounds over these coffins. Most mounds stood 2 to 3 feet (0.6 to 0.9 m) high. The largest were about 300 feet (90 m) in diameter and 70 feet (21 m) high.

Sandstone tablet from the Adena culture

GREAT ARTISTS

Meanwhile, another great Native American culture was taking root in the woodlands of the Ohio River valley. It is known as the Hopewell culture, named for a farmer in Ohio who owned the land where one of the mound complexes was located. Hopewell locations and mounds have led archaeologists to believe that this culture may have come from the Adena culture. The Hopewell people built larger mounds, and their culture also spread to Illinois and other places in the Midwest. Historians call the time from 800 BCE to 1200 CE, when the Adena and Hopewell cultures thrived, the Woodland Period.

The Hopewell culture developed around 100 BCE. At various Hopewell sites, archaeologists have found art objects made of copper, mica, seashells, and obsidian, a black volcanic glass. Analysis has shown that the copper came from deposits around Lake Superior, the mica from the southern Appalachian Mountains, the seashells from the Gulf of Mexico, and obsidian from the Rocky Mountains. Did the Hopewell people travel to these places or did they trade the material with people from other areas? Archaeologists do not yet know, but what is clear is that the Hopewell culture was not isolated from others.

Hopewell society was well organized. Many Hopewell people working together carried dirt to build the huge mounds and big earth walls all over the Ohio Valley. Archaeologists call mounds and other piles of dirt **earthworks**. The Hopewell earthworks are many different shapes—rectangles, circles, and squares.

Around 400 CE, the Hopewell culture disappeared. What happened to them? Did they die of disease? Did their food supplies run out? Were they killed by enemies?

A Hopewell ornament shaped like a bird's claw and made of mica

WORD TO KNOW

earthworks *works of art made from piled-up soil*

Mounds at the Hopewell Culture
National Historical Park

No one knows. Archaeologists do know that the children
and grandchildren of the Hopewell people stayed in the
Ohio Valley. Other groups came in from the north. A
new culture appeared to take the place of the Hopewell.
Archaeologists call it the Mississippian culture.

Building mounds and other earthworks was also
important to the Mississippian culture. These people
built earthworks shaped like birds and other animals.

A VERY BIG SNAKE

Imagine stumbling on a snake twisting through the
grass. What if that snake was 3.5 miles (5.6 km) long?
The first European explorers found just such a snake
on a bluff above the Little Miami River in what is now

An aerial view of Serpent Mound in Adams County

Q3 IF THE FORT ANCIENT PEOPLE HAD NO SHOVELS, HOW DID THEY DIG?

A3 The Fort Ancient people dug up dirt with bones. They used shoulder blades from deer and broad antlers from elk. They also used clamshells and sticks. They filled their baskets with 35 to 40 pounds (16 to 18 kilograms) of dirt and carried them to the mounds. The mounds that make up the snake vary from 4 to 23 feet (1.2 to 7 m) high.

Warren County. It was not a monster. It was a serpent-shaped mound of earth. Early European settlers in Ohio had seen thousands of mounds in the Ohio Valley. They thought the mounds had been used as forts. They named the serpent-shaped mound Fort Ancient.

This mound was built about 2,000 years ago, but its origin is unclear. Was it from the Hopewell culture or the Mississippian culture? Archaeologists are not sure. They call the society that built this mound the Fort Ancient culture.

Warren K. Moorehead was the first archaeologist to explore Fort Ancient in the late 1800s. He was awed by its size and by the people who built it. "Think of thousands of men and women toiling on the brow of this high hill with wicker baskets, skins, etc., piling up such an enormous earthwork by mere strength of hand and back," he wrote in 1890. "They had no shovels, no picks, no barrows; in fact, no tools at all, such as we use."

The Fort Ancient mound was not a fort at all. What was it? The prehistoric Native Americans did not have a written language. They left no records. Archaeologists have carefully looked for clues in the mound. They now believe that it was a giant clock. It did not tell time in hours. It told time in seasons. The Fort Ancient people watched the sun and moon move across the sky. Using mounds and gaps between the mounds, Fort Ancient people marked certain positions of the sun and moon. For example, the sun's rays lit up a certain mound on the morning of the summer solstice.

The people may have held religious ceremonies on the mound. In 2005, archaeologists found another mound nearby. They also found what looked like the ruins of houses. Did the ancient people live here?

There is an even larger grassy snake in Adams County. Serpent Mound is not as long as the Fort Ancient mound because it's a coiled snake. In area, however, it is the largest such mound in the world. No one knows for sure whether the people of the Fort Ancient culture also built this mound. A special kind of **carbon**, however, gives archaeologists a good clue.

Plants, animals, and everything alive contain a type of carbon called carbon 14. After death, the carbon 14 slowly changes into nitrogen. Objects, such as cloth or firewood, are made of things that were once alive. So they contain carbon 14. Scientists know the rate at

Picture Yourself . . .

at a Chunkey Game

If you were a child in a Fort Ancient village, you could cheer on your favorite player at a chunkey game. Men would throw poles at a special disk-shaped stone as it rolled along the ground. The man whose pole landed closest to the disk when it stopped rolling was the winner. The Fort Ancient people played chunkey only when their work was done. Everyone in the village worked hard at finding food and providing shelter. Boys and men fished with hooks made of bone. They hunted deer and other animals with bows and arrows. Girls and women grew fields of corn, bean, squash, and pumpkin. They cooked and stored food in clay pots. They made clothes by sewing hides together with a bone needle and thread made of sinews or plant fibers.

Chunkey disk

WORD TO KNOW

carbon *a chemical element found in all living things and things that were once alive*

Native American Peoples

(Before European Contact)

This map shows the general area of Native American peoples before European settlers arrived.

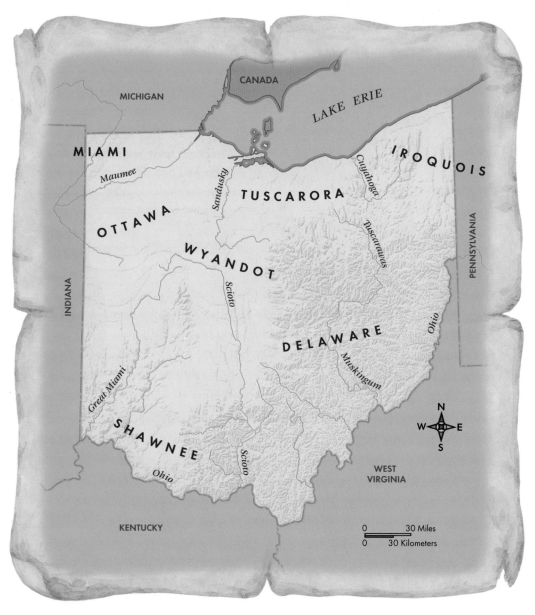

which carbon 14 changes. They use this as a clock to tell how old an object is. Archaeologists carbon-dated ashes from a wood fire found at Serpent Mound. The ashes dated between 1025 and 1215. This was the time of the Fort Ancient culture.

NEW GROUPS ARRIVE

The Mississippians had disappeared from Ohio by the mid-1600s. Archaeologists do not know why, but they have made some guesses. Perhaps these Native people used up the natural resources in the area. Also, it is possible that they knew from their trade contacts about the Europeans who had arrived in the eastern part of North America with their powerful guns and wanted to get away. More likely, the Mississippians died off from the new diseases that Europeans brought to America and that spread from one tribe to another well in advance of any European settlers. Weakened by disease, the survivors fled the area when the Iroquois of the New York area sought to control the Ohio country for the fur trade they carried on with the Europeans.

Between 40 and 60 years after they left, Native American groups from other areas moved in. Delawares, or Lenapes, came from the east. Wyandots, or Hurons, came from Canada. Shawnees moved up from the south, and Miamis came over from Indiana. Mingos, or Iroquois, traveled to Ohio from New York. These groups were settling in Ohio when early Europeans began to arrive.

MINI-BIO

BARBARA ALICE MANN: NATIVE AMERICAN AUTHOR

Barbara Alice Mann (1947–) has dedicated herself to studying the history of her Seneca (Iroquois) ancestors and telling the story of Native Americans who lived in her home state of Ohio. Most North American history books are written by European Americans. Mann looks at North American history through Native American eyes. The difference is somewhat like a story told by two different people. Mann shares the way she as a Native American understands history by writing books. She also teaches at the University of Toledo.

? **Want to know more?** See www.utoledo.edu/as/english/people/mann.html

WOW

You can see ancient Native American "graffiti" on a rock on Kelleys Island in Lake Erie. The pictures of animals and people were carved into Inscription Rock between 1200 and 1600.

READ ABOUT

Explorer René-Robert Cavelier, Sieur de La Salle, claiming land for France

1670

French explorer René-Robert Cavelier, Sieur de La Salle, reaches Ohio

1754

The French and Indian War begins

▲**1763–1764**

Pontiac leads Native Americans in a rebellion

CHAPTER THREE

EXPLORATION AND SETTLEMENT

★

IN 1670, FRENCH EXPLORERS ARRIVED IN OHIO. They were under the leadership of René-Robert Cavelier, Sieur de La Salle. The Europeans were looking for a waterway that could carry ships to Asia. Trade between China and Europe was booming. The ships bringing silks and spices from China to Europe had to make the long journey around Africa. La Salle had heard about the Ohio River and hoped it might be a shortcut.

1788

Marietta, Ohio's first permanent white settlement, is founded

1794

Native Americans are defeated in the Battle of Fallen Timbers

1795 ▶

The Treaty of Greenville is signed

EXPLORATION AND SETTLEMENT

European Exploration of Ohio

The colored arrows on this map show the routes taken by explorers between 1670 and 1820.

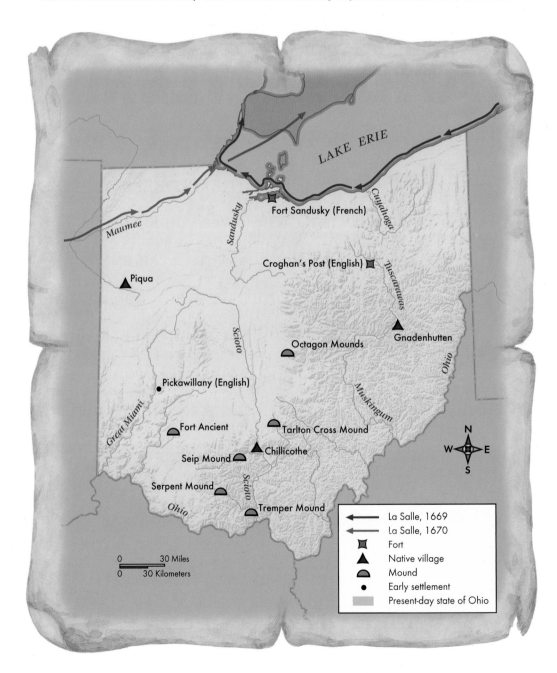

LAKE ERIE

Maumee

Sandusky

Cuyahoga

Fort Sandusky (French)

Croghan's Post (English)

Tuscarawas

Piqua

Scioto

Octagon Mounds

Gnadenhutten

Ohio

Pickawillany (English)

Great Miami

Muskingum

Fort Ancient

Tarlton Cross Mound

Seip Mound

Chillicothe

Serpent Mound

Scioto

Ohio

Tremper Mound

N W E S

| 0 | 30 Miles |
| 0 | 30 Kilometers |

La Salle, 1669
La Salle, 1670
Fort
Native village
Mound
Early settlement
Present-day state of Ohio

THE BEAVER FUR TRADE

La Salle must have been disappointed to find that the Ohio River was not a shortcut across North America, since it does not flow into the Pacific Ocean. He went on to explore the Mississippi River. Other explorers were not disappointed. They saw something of great value in Ohio—beavers.

Beaver fur might bring them more riches than silks and spices from China. Coats and tall hats made of beaver fur were fashionable in Europe in the 1700s, and wealthy people were willing to pay a lot of money for the furs. Millions of beavers played and splashed in Ohio's rivers. Native Americans trapped and skinned the beavers and sold the pelts to European fur traders.

Native Americans used muskets and bows and arrows to hunt beavers in Ohio rivers.

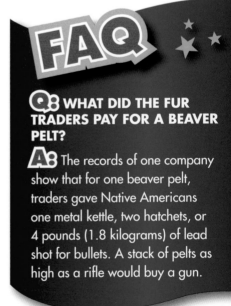

FAQ

Q8 WHAT DID THE FUR TRADERS PAY FOR A BEAVER PELT?

A8 The records of one company show that for one beaver pelt, traders gave Native Americans one metal kettle, two hatchets, or 4 pounds (1.8 kilograms) of lead shot for bullets. A stack of pelts as high as a rifle would buy a gun.

Picture Yourself . . .

on a Fur-Trading Trip

If you were the child of an early fur trader who journeyed to Ohio, your father might be French and your mother a Miami. If you were a girl, your mother might make you a long deerskin dress. If you were a boy, your mother might make you a jacket of deerskin. Boys and girls both had chores to do. They helped gather and pack food and other supplies for trips to get furs. If you were a boy, your father might take you on a fur-trading trip. You would travel Ohio's rivers by canoe to Native American villages. At night, you would camp along the riverbanks and sleep under the stars. If you were a girl, you stayed at the trading post with your mother. You learned to plant crops, cook food, and make clothes of deerskin and cloth.

WORD TO KNOW

colony *a community settled in a new land but with ties to another government*

George Washington helped start the French and Indian War in 1754, when he and his Virginia troops attacked the French fort located where the city of Pittsburgh is today. At that time, he was an officer in the British army of Virginia with the assignment to drive the French out of the Ohio Valley.

The fur trade in North America started on the East Coast. By the mid-1600s, Iroquois groups had trapped so many beavers for the New York fur trade that the number of beavers dropped significantly. The Iroquois then moved into the Ohio River valley in search of a new beaver supply. Europeans came to Ohio for the same reason.

THE FRENCH AND INDIAN WAR

The British and French competed for the fur trade. France declared that the Ohio River valley was part of its **colony**, New France, and wanted all British people to stay east of the Appalachian Mountains. British fur traders, mostly from Pennsylvania, ignored the French and continued to conduct a vigorous business. Meanwhile, King George II of Great Britain told people living in Virginia that they could have the land in the Ohio Valley for farming. In 1754, when the French built a fort at the source of the Ohio River to block British traders and settlers from entering the area, war soon broke out between England and France.

Some Native American groups sided with the British, while others sided with the French. The war, from 1754 to 1763, was known as the French and Indian War in America. Most of the battles fought in North America occurred east of Ohio and north into Canada. In the end, the British won, and France gave up its claim to Canada and all land from the Mississippi River eastward to the Appalachian Mountains, including Ohio.

PONTIAC: UNITING NATIVE AMERICANS

Born to an Ottawa father and an Ojibwe mother, Pontiac (c. 1720–1769) believed that Native Americans were losing land to Europeans because the Native Americans had displeased the gods by abandoning traditional beliefs and adopting European ways. When the British gained control of the Ohio Valley in 1763, Pontiac urged Native American groups to unite. They attacked British forts and settlements in a short war known as Pontiac's Rebellion. When British troops put down the uprising in 1764, Pontiac made peace.

 Want to know more? See www.ohiohistorycentral.org/entry.php?rec=306

Native Americans meeting with Colonel Henry Bouquet, an English officer, in 1764, near what is now Bolivar, Ohio

Native groups in Ohio were disturbed that the British had won, because the British planned to bring in more settlers. Settlers cut down trees and turned the forests into farm fields. Destroying Ohio's forests would destroy the Native American hunting grounds.

A great Ottawa chief named Pontiac wanted to drive the British out of the Ohio River valley and the land around the Great Lakes and the Mississippi River. In 1763, the same year the French and Indian War ended, Pontiac called on other groups of Native Americans to rebel against the British. The Native Americans fought bravely. They hoped that the French would help them as they had helped the French. When the French failed to send the Native Americans guns and ammunition, the Indians were forced to give up the fight.

The French and Indian War was part of a bigger war in Europe. There it was called the Seven Years' War and involved many countries.

SEE IT HERE!

SCHOENBRUNN VILLAGE STATE MEMORIAL

What did an Ohio school look like before the Revolutionary War? You can see for yourself at Schoenbrunn Village State Memorial in New Philadelphia. **Missionaries** from Germany built the village in 1772 to convert Delaware people to Christianity. About 400 Delawares moved into the village. It grew to have more than 60 homes, a church, and the school. You will see 17 buildings made to look just like the originals. Guides in costumes will show you what life was like.

WORD TO KNOW

missionaries *people who try to convert others to a religion*

THE UNITED STATES CLAIMS THE LAND

In 1775, the 13 British colonies on the East Coast rebelled against Great Britain. By 1783, they had won their independence and formed the United States of America. The new nation claimed the Ohio country, which had been held by the British. In 1787, the United States passed the Northwest Ordinance, which established the Northwest Territory. This territory stretched from the Ohio River to the Canadian border and from the Appalachian Mountains to the Mississippi River. It included what are now Ohio, Indiana, Michigan, Illinois, Wisconsin, and part of Minnesota.

Pioneers on the Ohio River settling the old Northwest Territory, late 1700s

The beginnings of Marietta, a settlement founded in 1788

The Northwest Ordinance set up a process by which a territory could become a state, equal to the original states. This meant that the frontier region would not be a permanent colony of the national government. Instead, it would be an equal member of the nation. No other nation in the world had ever done this with its territory before. The Northwest Ordinance also forbade the introduction of slavery into the territory and required that public schools be established.

EARLY SETTLERS

In 1788, a group of New Englanders purchased a tract of land along the Ohio River. They named their settlement Marietta, and it was the first permanent white settlement in what would become Ohio. Marietta served as the capital of the Northwest Territory for one winter before the capital was moved down the Ohio River to the area that became Cincinnati.

General "Mad Anthony" Wayne's forces at the Battle of Fallen Timbers on the banks of the Maumee River

Other settlers in Ohio were Revolutionary War veterans who were given land as payment for their military service. In the 1780s and early 1790s, some veterans cleared and farmed land in the Ohio River valley. But overall, Ohio had few settlers, particularly in the north. Native Americans had never agreed to the terms of the treaty in which the British granted the Americans this land. They discouraged white settlement by attacking the newcomers who threatened their way of life.

CONTINUING TROUBLE

Meanwhile, the British held on to some forts in what is now Ohio and Michigan, despite their agreement with the United States to leave the area. The Native Americans hoped the British would help them fight the American settlers and U.S. troops. Little Turtle, a Miami warrior and leader, organized Native American groups to resist the settlers. First Little Turtle and then

Blue Jacket, a Shawnee, led the Native warriors to major victories over U.S. troops in 1790 and 1791.

President George Washington was upset by these losses and brought in General "Mad Anthony" Wayne, a top military leader in the Revolutionary War. In 1794, Wayne led U.S. troops against Native Americans in the Battle of Fallen Timbers, a spot where a tornado had blown down many trees. The Indians crouched down and hid behind the fallen trees and then attacked the U.S. troops. But Wayne drove the Native Americans back. They fled to a British fort, in hopes that the British would let them in and protect them. The British refused, and the Indians were forced to surrender.

Native American leaders signed a peace treaty with the United States called the Treaty of Greenville the following year. They agreed to move their people to the northwestern corner of Ohio and to land farther west. But not all Native Americans agreed to the treaty, and the threat of renewed fighting in Ohio continued for another 20 years. Still, the defeat of the Native Americans at Fallen Timbers and the signing of the Treaty of Greenville encouraged settlers to swarm into the area and opened up the northeast part of the state. For instance, Cleveland was settled in 1796.

MINI-BIO

LITTLE TURTLE: NATIVE AMERICAN LEADER

Little Turtle (1752?–1812), or Michikinikwa, was a great leader of the Miami nation. He helped the British in the Revolutionary War. He then led warriors in trying to keep U.S. settlers out of Ohio. He won great military victories, and young warriors looked up to him. When he asked the British to help him and they refused, he knew the Native Americans could not win the struggle. He refused to lead warriors in the Battle of Fallen Timbers. He urged his people to live in peace with the settlers.

? **Want to know more?** See www. ohiohistorycentral.org/image. php?rec=240&img=151

The signatures of General Wayne and Native American leaders on the Treaty of Greenville

1796
Cleveland is founded

▲**1803**
Ohio becomes a state

1812
Columbus becomes the state capital

CHAPTER FOUR

GROWTH AND CHANGE

★

Aftter the revolutionary war, some people saw the ohio valley as a place to get rich. Land companies bought millions of acres from the federal government and the state of Connecticut, which claimed land along Lake Erie. These companies sold the land to settlers for much more than they paid for it.

1833
The Ohio and Erie Canal is completed

1871
B. F. Goodrich becomes the first rubber company in Akron

early 1900 ►
Ohio women work for voting rights

Settlers traveling by flatboat down the Ohio River, early 1800s

SETTLEMENT AND STATEHOOD

The Ohio Company of Associates laid out Ohio's first town, Marietta, in 1788, and the Connecticut Land Company founded Cleveland in 1796. But Ohio was hard to get to, and settlers feared Indian attacks. Marietta at first attracted only 48 settlers. By 1800, only three settlers had bought land in Cleveland.

Other **speculators** founded a town where the Licking River joined the Ohio River. Because of its location on two rivers, the town, which came to be called Cincinnati, grew faster than other Ohio communities. It had about 1,000 residents by 1803. Most newcomers to Ohio came by boat and settled along the Ohio River. Many early settlers came by flatboat, a big raft with wooden sides that could carry one family and its possessions. When a family reached its destination, family members broke the boat apart and used the wood to build their new home.

WORD TO KNOW

speculators *people who buy land or other items and hope to sell for more than they paid*

Ohio: From Territory to Statehood
(1787–1803)

This map shows the original Northwest Territory and the area (outlined in red) that became the state of Ohio in 1803.

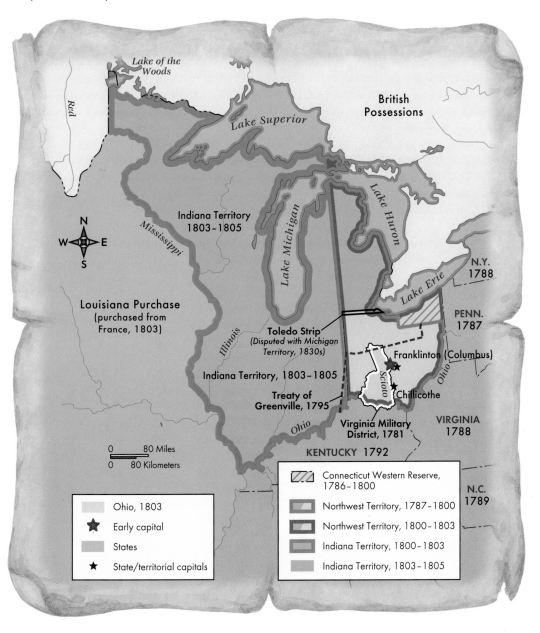

By 1803, enough people had settled in Ohio for it to become the 17th state to join the Union. Its capital was Chillicothe, in the south-central part of the state. Legislators later decided to move the capital to a more central location, so they built a new town called Columbus. About 4,000 people called Columbus home by 1834.

MORE NATIVE AMERICAN RESISTANCE

A Shawnee leader named Tecumseh watched as speculators sold land in Ohio and other places. In 1795, he had refused to sign the Treaty of Greenville. "These lands are ours," he wrote to President James Madison in 1810. "The Great Spirit above has appointed the place for us, on which to light our fires, and here we will remain." Tecumseh believed that the best defense against the invasion of settlers would be to unite Native American groups into a single **confederation**. He and his brother, who was known as the Prophet, set up a village called Prophet's Town near the Tippecanoe River in Indiana Territory.

WORD TO KNOW

confederation *an association of groups that come together with common goals*

A scene from the Battle of Tippecanoe in 1811

Many Native Americans traveled to the village from Ohio, Kentucky, and Indiana Territory. When territorial governor William Henry Harrison learned of the growing gathering, he led U.S. troops to the village. Tecumseh was away, recruiting more Indians for the cause. He had left the Prophet behind with orders not to attack the Americans. But the Prophet had a vision that told him to lead warriors into battle. Although Harrison lost more men at the Battle of Tippecanoe, the Native Americans were defeated.

Tecumseh did not give up. When war broke out between Great Britain and the United States in 1812, Tecumseh and his followers sided with the British. Tecumseh was killed in battle. The confederation he had dreamed of was broken up forever.

CANALS AND OTHER CONNECTIONS

By 1812, British troops still had not left the Northwest Territory. They encouraged Native Americans to attack American settlers. Great Britain also continued to cause trouble by interfering with U.S. shipping and trade in the Atlantic Ocean. The War of 1812 broke out over these issues. After the two sides became stalemated and made peace, Ohio began to grow rapidly. Better forms of transportation helped bring settlers to farms and towns all over the Ohio Valley.

The first transportation routes to Ohio were rivers, with the Ohio River being most important. There were no major roads, just trails that had to be walked because a rider sitting tall in the saddle was constantly bothered by low branches and brush. Early river travel also posed problems because while a boat could easily float downstream, it was very difficult to move it upstream.

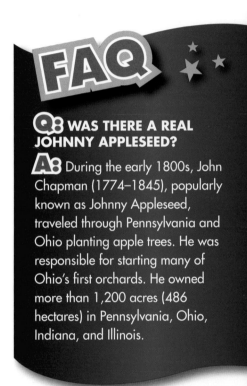

FAQ

Q8 WAS THERE A REAL JOHNNY APPLESEED?

A8 During the early 1800s, John Chapman (1774–1845), popularly known as Johnny Appleseed, traveled through Pennsylvania and Ohio planting apple trees. He was responsible for starting many of Ohio's first orchards. He owned more than 1,200 acres (486 hectares) in Pennsylvania, Ohio, Indiana, and Illinois.

This print shows a bridge over the Erie Canal, 1840s.

AFRICAN AMERICAN SEAMEN

Captain Oliver Perry won a great sea victory on Lake Erie during the War of 1812. One out of four of his seamen was African American.

This was solved in 1811, when the *New Orleans* became the first steamboat to travel up the Ohio River from the Mississippi. In 1818, the steamboat *Walk-in-the-Water* began carrying passengers and goods on Lake Erie.

In 1806, Congress authorized building the National Road, the first "modern" federal highway, in order to link the middle part of Ohio and places to the west to the nation's East Coast. The new road, along with the completion in 1825 of the Erie Canal, greatly improved east-west travel to the state.

To ship farm products and manufactured goods to more places more efficiently, Ohio built a number of canals in the 1800s. The first canal, the Ohio and Erie Canal, was completed in 1833 and connected Cleveland on Lake Erie with Portsmouth on the Ohio River. About 4,000 people worked to build several other canals, which allowed Ohioans to ship farm products and factory goods cheaply from the Atlantic Ocean to the Gulf of Mexico. New cities and towns, such as Akron, sprang up along the canals.

Even before the canals were finished, however, a new way of shipping goods and transporting people was being created—railroads. Sending goods on a canal barge pulled by mules walking on a towpath was cheap, but slow. The trip between Cleveland and Portsmouth took almost three and a half days. A train trip was more expensive, but it was much faster. Railroads could also serve towns that were not connected by canals.

In the late 1800s, small electric trains began connecting one community with another. These railroads were called **interurbans**. Ohioans built the first interurban line in the United States. It ran between Newark and Granville.

AFRICAN AMERICANS IN OHIO

When Ohio became a state, its constitution made slavery illegal, but it also denied African American citizens the right to vote. Black men could not serve on juries or testify against white people. African American children could not attend public schools.

In 1807, the Ohio legislature passed laws aimed at keeping African Americans out of the state, but these regulations were rarely enforced. Ohio became a refuge for free blacks or people fleeing slavery, some of whom founded black communities.

There was friction among Cincinnati's blacks, Cincinnati's whites dependent on trade with the slave South, and slaveholders who crossed over from Kentucky to capture runaway slaves. In 1848, an armed slave-hunting posse arrived from Kentucky. Black Cincinnati housewives wielding shovels, washboards, and rolling pins drove them off. Despite being hounded

By the early 1900s, interurban railways connected most Ohio cities and towns.

WORD TO KNOW

interurbans *small trains or trolley cars connecting two or more cities*

SEE IT HERE!

THE OLD OHIO AND ERIE CANAL

A section of the Ohio and Erie Canal still exists at a place called Roscoe Village. The village has been restored to show what life was like in the 1830s. During the summer, horses walking along the towpath pull a restored barge through the canal.

MINI-BIO

HARRIET BEECHER STOWE: ACTIVIST AUTHOR

Harriet Beecher Stowe (1811–1893) lived in Cincinnati when she wrote her best-selling book of the 1850s, Uncle Tom's Cabin. She interviewed and aided escapees who crossed the Ohio River from Kentucky. She based her book about the evils of slavery on true stories of the people she met. When she met President Abraham Lincoln during the Civil War, he reportedly said, "So you're the little woman who wrote the book that started this Great War!" Today, her house on Gilbert Avenue in Cincinnati celebrates the brave men and women she helped and the author who championed their cause.

? Want to know more? See www.ohiohistorycentral. org/entry.php?rec=360

WORD TO KNOW

abolitionists *people who were opposed to slavery and worked to end it*

by slave hunters, Cincinnati's black community grew. By the end of the 1840s, African Americans owned their own homes, factories, and stores. By 1860, the black community in Cincinnati ran five schools, five churches, 11 self-help societies and cultural centers, and an orphanage.

During this time, Ohio had 20 to 30 all-black towns. Education was important to African Americans arriving in Ohio. One black colony in Mercer County boasted that its 70 families each owned farms of 20 to 40 acres (8 to 16 ha), were better educated than white communities, and had "the best library of books in northwestern Ohio." In 1835, Oberlin College became the first college in the nation to admit both male and female African American students—as well as white women—on an equal standing with white, male students. By the 1850s, Antioch College also admitted African Americans and women.

Many white **abolitionists** lived in Ohio. From the time Ohio became a state, they were ready to help people escaping slavery. For example, in 1808, an enslaved Virginian named Jane was sentenced to death for stealing four dollars' worth of goods from a Charleston store. White people helped her escape to Marietta. When Virginians tried to arrest Jane, her new Ohio friends protected her.

This spot on the Ohio River, near Steubenville, was a crossing point for escaped slaves on the Underground Railroad.

In 1841, the state supreme court declared Ohio a safe refuge for escapees. In 1850, however, the U.S. Congress passed a law that allowed slaveholders to recapture slaves in any Free State. The only safe place for fleeing African Americans was Canada. Many escaped through the Underground Railroad, a system of trails and hiding places for African Americans making their way to freedom.

Both black and white people served as conductors on the Underground Railroad, guiding escapees all the way to Canada. Ohio had 1,540 Underground Railroad stations and produced many of its daring conductors. Sojourner Truth, who had escaped slavery, spent two years driving her horse-drawn buggy along the Ohio River, persuading white farm families to help the runaways who crossed over to their shores. From 1830 to 1860, at least 40,000 men, women, and children escaped bondage through Ohio. Some African Americans chose to stay in Ohio. Just before the Civil War (1861–1865), about 37,000 blacks lived in the state.

Oberlin College stood at the juncture of five different routes of the Underground Railroad. It was, one

UNDERGROUND TEAMWORK

John Rankin (1793–1886) was a Presbyterian minister and an abolitionist. He risked his life to help enslaved people escape from slaveholders in the South. From outside his home in Ripley along the Ohio River, he used a lantern to signal runaways in Kentucky that it was safe to cross over. He helped about 2,000 enslaved persons escape.

His black neighbor John Parker often brought the African Americans over on a boat. Parker, a former enslaved person, confronted slave-hunting posses and "never thought of going uptown without a pistol in my pocket, a knife in my belt, and a blackjack handy." One night, while helping a group of runaways flee Kentucky, Parker lit a match and saw on a tree a poster reading: "REWARD $1,000 FOR JOHN PARKER, DEAD OR ALIVE." He never stopped his work.

slave hunter complained, "an old buzzard's nest where the Negroes who arrive over the underground railroad are regarded as dear children." Cincinnati was another important place for stops on the Underground Railroad. In 1847, Levi Coffin and his wife, Catherine, moved from Indiana to Cincinnati to help fugitives. Coffin earned the title "the president of the Underground Railroad" for helping an estimated 3,000 enslaved people escape.

In addition to Underground Railroad conductors, Ohio produced antislavery politicians and newspaper publishers. Rutherford B. Hayes, who later became a U.S. president, served as an attorney for runaways.

THE CIVIL WAR AND AFTER

Not everyone in Ohio wanted to see slavery end, especially Ohioans from Southern states. When the Civil War broke out in 1861, Ohio's citizens were divided on the issue of slavery. Yet Ohio fought on the side of the Union and played a key role in its victory. More than 300,000 Ohio troops, including 5,000 African Americans, volunteered to fight. The major commanders for the North were Ohioans, including generals Grant, Sherman, and Sheridan. President Abraham Lincoln's cabinet included a number of Ohioans, such as Salmon Chase as secretary of the treasury and Edwin M. Stanton as secretary of war.

Many Ohio troops died or suffered severe wounds during the Civil War. One of these soldiers was Robert H. Caldwell. He wrote to his father from a battlefield in Tennessee in January 1863, "I was obliged to retreat from the field in consequence of a wound received in my left shoulder. The missile was a round musket ball. . . . It was taken out by a surgeon. . . . It is but a slight wound and in all probability I shall be roving again in a few weeks." But infection set in, and Caldwell became one of more than 11,000 Ohio soldiers to die of wounds.

Before the Civil War ended in 1865, Ohio's African Americans began working to gain full citizenship. They helped form the National Equal Rights League. They pushed for passage in 1868 of the 14th Amendment to the U.S. Constitution that promised equal rights under the law for all persons. Feelings over the 14th Amendment were so strong that Ohio at first ratified it and then a year later tried to rescind its approval. Ohio at first rejected the 15th Amendment, guaranteeing all citizens the right to vote, but then narrowly approved it in 1870. Despite several tries, Ohio did not amend its own constitution to allow African Americans to vote until 1923, although in practice blacks did vote.

OHIO SUFFRAGETTES

After the Civil War, many Ohio women who had been abolitionists turned their attention to women's rights. They had hoped that the 14th and 15th amendments to the U.S. Constitution would give them the right to vote, known as suffrage, but this did not happen. They held parades and demonstrations in favor of suffrage. Because of this, they became known as **suffragettes**. Finally, in 1920, the 19th Amendment to the Constitution granted them suffrage.

HALLIE Q. BROWN: TEACHER AND ACTIVIST

Born to former slaves before the Civil War, Hallie Q. Brown (1845–1949) graduated in 1873 from Wilberforce University, a school for African Americans. She became a leading educator in Dayton public schools. She began to hold lectures in the United States and Europe. In 1900, she took up the cause of woman suffrage, carrying the message of full citizenship for all, regardless of color. Brown served as president of the National Association of Colored Women in the 1920s.

? Want to know more? See voices.cla.umn.edu/vg/Bios/entries/brown_hallie_quinn.html

WORD TO KNOW

suffragettes *women in the early 1900s who worked for women's right to vote*

A postcard from 1915

GROWING INDUSTRY

Powered by steam engines, industry grew rapidly in Ohio after the Civil War. Steam engines required coal, which was plentiful in eastern and southern Ohio. Thousands of miners, many of them immigrants from Wales or Ireland, arrived to remove coal from the earth.

Industry also needed iron. Before the Civil War, iron makers would find a spot that had everything they needed to produce it: iron ore and limestone, and charcoal to heat the ore. They dug the ore and limestone from the ground and burned trees to make charcoal. When these raw materials were used up, the iron makers moved to a new location. After the Civil War, iron production moved to foundries in the northeastern part of the state. Iron companies replaced charcoal with coal and made steel from iron. By the 1890s, Ohio ranked second among the states in steel production.

Automobile manufacturing also began in Ohio in the late 1800s. Many of Ohio's small automakers became part of General Motors when the auto industry moved to Detroit, Michigan. The auto industry, however, brought a new industry to Ohio—tire manufacturing. The B. F. Goodrich Company was already making rubber in Akron for fire hoses. The Firestone Tire and Rubber Company was making rubber buggy tires. The Goodyear Tire & Rubber Company was also there. All these companies switched to making auto tires, and Akron became the "rubber capital of the world."

Industrial growth brought great wealth to factory and mine owners and investors. Ordinary workers, however, were not paid or treated well. Miners worked in dark tunnels or in open pits doing dangerous work. Most lived in houses owned by the mines and shopped at company stores. Many miners were charged more than they earned for food and housing, and they fell deep into debt to the companies they worked for. A miner might work 12 to 14 hours a day and earn less than a dollar. Factory workers also suffered from long hours, low pay, and terrible working conditions.

The American Federation of Labor was founded in Columbus in 1886 and the United Mine Workers was founded four years later. In 1898, the **union** won an eight-hour workday for miners.

IMMIGRATION

Before the Civil War, most of Ohio's immigrants came from Germany. The next largest groups of immigrants came from England and Ireland. After the Civil War, Ohio's population grew rapidly. Between 1870 and 1910, Ohio gained more than 2 million new residents. Newcomers came from Italy, Hungary, Poland, Russia, Czechoslovakia, and other southern and eastern European countries. Many settled in Cleveland and other places along Lake Erie. Each immigrant group formed its own community. They held on to their own

WORD TO KNOW

union *an organization formed by workers to try to improve working conditions and wages*

Workers at National Machinery's metalworking plant in Tiffin, early 1900s

cultural traditions, spoke their native languages, and gathered in their own places of worship. But slowly over decades, as the children of the immigrants went to public schools, learned English, socialized and played sports with their peers, interacted in the workplace, and eventually married spouses from other ethnic communities, the immigrant culture of the parents faded but never fully disappeared.

PROGRESSIVE REFORM

In the short run, industrialism produced tremendous social problems that local and state governments were not used to dealing with. Overcrowded cities featured firetrap housing, polluted water, and no system for the safe removal of trash and other waste. Factories lacked proper ventilation and machines had few safety features, resulting in high accident rates. The growth of big business created huge disparities, or differences, in wealth and influence that made people wonder if political democracy could survive in the face of growing economic inequity, or unfairness.

Beginning in the 1890s, leaders in Ohio's cities were at the forefront of the nation in addressing these problems in what became known as the Progressive Movement. In Toledo, Samuel "Golden Rule" Jones initiated reforms such as building public parks, paving roads, and regulating streetcar fares. In Cleveland, the popular mayor Tom Johnson followed Jones's example and improved the city's water supply and redesigned the downtown area to make it more livable. In 1912, the state's voters approved a number of progressive amendments to the Ohio constitution that improved the cities, reformed the workplace, and encouraged more popular participation in government.

AT WAR, AGAIN

The United States entered World War I (1914–1918) in 1917. Most Ohioans did what they could to help the war effort. More than 200,000 Ohioans served in the military during this time. About 6,500 Ohio soldiers were killed in battle. On the home front, Ohio's mines, factories, and farms dramatically increased production in order to equip American and allied soldiers and feed and clothe the millions of refugees in war-torn Europe. The Ohio Industrial Commission supplied workers for war-related jobs and sent college students to help out in farm fields to ensure an adequate food supply.

Historians consider World War I to be the first modern war, using new kinds of tactics and weapons. Soldiers fought for months in wet, muddy trenches. They faced attacks with poison gas. About 9 million soldiers on both sides died. When the war ended in 1918, people in Ohio, like other Americans, were glad the conflict was over. Ohioans were ready for a new age to begin.

The 372nd Infantry Regiment, which included African American troops from Ohio, marching on Broad Street in Columbus after the end of World War I

1930

Cleveland's African American population rises to 72,000

▲ **1940s**

Women work in Ohio factories during World War II

1959

The St. Lawrence Seaway opens

CHAPTER FIVE

MORE MODERN TIMES

★

AFTER WORLD WAR I, OHIOANS LEFT THEIR FARMS FOR JOBS IN CITIES. Freighters brought iron ore from Lake Superior to Toledo, Cleveland, and Youngstown. Mills turned the ore into iron and steel. Factory workers turned out parts for new inventions, such as cars and airplanes. The state continued to supply coal for industry and began providing natural gas and oil. Ohio became the heart of the U.S. manufacturing region.

1960s
Civil rights protests are held across Ohio

◄ **1967**
Cleveland elects Carl Burton Stokes the first African American mayor of a major U.S. city

2001
A new Jeep plant opens in Toledo

The Wright brothers with one of their airplanes at Simms Station in 1904

In 1927, Cleveland Hopkins International became the first municipal airport and air traffic control tower.

THE ROARING TWENTIES

People born in Ohio had invented things that were changing the world by the 1920s. Orville and Wilbur Wright made the first working airplane in a bicycle shop in Dayton. They flew it in 1903. By the 1920s, the airplane had caught on.

Milan-born Thomas A. Edison invented a number of devices in the 1880s that had totally changed life by the 1920s. People listened to records played on his phonograph. They laughed and cried at movies made with his cameras and projectors. His lightbulbs lit up buildings and homes. In the 1890s, Cleveland was the first city to switch from gas lamps to electric streetlights.

Young people loved to dance to lively jazz music, made popular by phonograph records and radio. Across the country, people bought 100 million jazz and other records in 1927 alone. In cities and small towns, Ohioans could hear great jazz musicians such as Count Basie, Duke Ellington, and Fats Waller.

In Ohio cities, people flocked to movie palaces such as the State Theater in Cleveland's Playhouse Square. Baseball fans cheered on the Cincinnati Reds. Each year, they hoped the team would win the World Series as they had in 1919.

Young people in the 1920s saw Cleveland as the place to be. Many companies in Cleveland made the newest high-tech devices for the home. Electric batteries, vacuum cleaners, radios, coffee percolators, hot plates, kitchen ranges, hair dryers, and electric heaters rolled out of Cleveland factories.

Heavy industry also boomed during the 1920s. Iron and steel mills belched smoke into the air around cities such as Youngstown. "Everybody breathing dirt, eating dirt . . . they call it 'pay dirt,' for Youngstown clean would be Youngstown out of work," said labor leader Frank Bohn.

Most African Americans did not fare nearly as well as whites. But they made some progress during the 1920s. Beginning with World War I, thousands of African Americans moved from the South to northern cities in what is called the Great Migration. The black population of Cleveland increased from about 10,000 during World War I to 72,000 by 1930. They took the lowest-paying jobs in industry. African Americans still were denied equal rights in housing, jobs, and education. Many lived in **ghettos**. They attended black churches. They read black newspapers, which

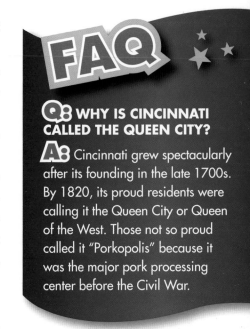

Q8 WHY IS CINCINNATI CALLED THE QUEEN CITY?

A8 Cincinnati grew spectacularly after its founding in the late 1700s. By 1820, its proud residents were calling it the Queen City or Queen of the West. Those not so proud called it "Porkopolis" because it was the major pork processing center before the Civil War.

WORD TO KNOW

ghettos *slum areas of cities occupied by disadvantaged people*

MINI-BIO

HARRY C. SMITH: CRUSADING EDITOR

Harry C. Smith (1863–1941) helped found *The Cleveland Gazette*, an African American newspaper. As editor, he used his newspaper to fight for civil rights and broadcast his political views. He was elected to the Ohio legislature in 1893, where he introduced the Smith Act, one of the strictest laws against lynching. He also pushed for passage of the Ohio Civil Rights Law of 1894. After leaving politics, he returned to journalism. He died while at work in his newspaper office.

? Want to know more? See www.ohiohistorycentral.org/entry.php?rec=345

WORDS TO KNOW

civil rights *basic human rights that all citizens in a society are entitled to, such as the right to vote*

lynching *to kill by mob without a lawful trial*

stocks *shares in the ownership of a company*

printed stories about wrongs committed against blacks by the Ku Klux Klan, a violent group that believed whites were superior to blacks. "Say what you may, think what you will, the fact remains that the Ku Klux Klan is ever busy, ever growing. . . . They work while you sleep," warned an April 1923 issue of *The Union*, Cincinnati's black newspaper.

FROM GOOD TIMES TO BAD TIMES

At the end of the 1920s, industrial production began to slow down. Prices for farm products were low. Then came the stock market crash of October 1929, which made many **stocks** worthless. The crash of 1929 and other serious economic problems set off the Great Depression of the 1930s.

People lost their jobs as companies went out of business. By 1932, more than 37 percent of all workers in Ohio were unemployed. People who were able to keep their jobs also faced hard times. Some worked fewer hours or had their pay cut. Schools were not able to pay their teachers, and some lost their homes. People stopped paying their doctors, grocers, and landlords. Those who could not find work became desperate to feed their families.

During the Depression, workers in the mass production industries formed unions to help them win some protection from being fired or laid off, as well

Police clash with strikers from the Goodyear Tire & Rubber Company in Akron.

as better pay and working conditions. Sometimes, the workers went on **strike** to force the business owners to talk to them.

Rubber workers in Akron formed the United Rubber Workers union in 1935. When, in the cold winter of 1936, the Goodyear Tire & Rubber Company refused to talk to union representatives about the workers' grievances, the workers marched out of the plant and established a huge picket line encircling the tire works. The strike dragged on for many weeks, but was finally settled in the union's favor. It was the first major victory for a new national labor federation called the Congress of Industrial Organizations.

WORD TO KNOW

strike *an organized refusal to work, usually as a sign of protest about working conditions*

Ohio experienced other dramatic strikes, like the 1934 uprising of the Toledo Auto-Lite workers. In late 1936, workers at Cleveland's Fisher Body plant launched a sit-down strike, in which they stayed inside the plant rather than picket outside. The new unions did not win all the strikes. Workers at Youngstown Steel and Republic Steel suffered major defeats in 1937. Still, the growth of unions in Ohio in the 1930s is important because unions gave workers an increased say about the terms they worked under, they helped raise workers' incomes, and they organized workers into a powerful block of voters.

Franklin D. Roosevelt became president of the United States in 1933. He had a plan called the New Deal for helping people cope with the Great Depression. To do this, he had to change the relationship between the states and the national government that had existed since the Revolution. New Deal programs brought federal relief to thousands of Ohioans through programs that hired people to construct bridges, roads, dams, parks, and even the Toledo Zoo. Various banking and other economic reforms helped the U.S. economy begin to recover. Although the New Deal initiated programs such as Social Security to help retired people in need, the widespread unemployment caused by the Great Depression did not end until World War II began.

OHIO DURING WORLD WAR II

World War II began in Europe in 1939 when Germany invaded Poland. The United States did not enter the war until after the Japanese bombed the U.S. naval base at Pearl Harbor in Hawai'i on December 7, 1941. Germany and Japan were on the same side in the conflict.

The United States and its **allies**—Great Britain, France, and Russia—needed steel for tanks and other

WORD TO KNOW

allies *nations that are on the same side in a conflict*

Workers at the airplane division of Curtiss-Wright Corporation in Columbus during World War II

weapons. War vehicles needed rubber for tires. Suddenly, there was plenty of work. Ohio women stepped up to fill the jobs as 839,000 Ohioans, mostly men, went off to war. The women welded airplane frames and molded bullets. Before World War II, they had been barred from many kinds of jobs and were paid much less than men. During World War II, Ohio's women workers were treated equal to men. They played a major role in helping the United States and its allies win the war. The state's African Americans, both male and female, also were able to get jobs that formerly were denied them.

THE FIFTIES

Ohio industry continued to grow after the war ended in 1945. By then, two-thirds of all the world's steel came from mills in the United States. With jobs plentiful and wages high, most Ohioans experienced a prosperity that their parents had never known.

Transportation played a major role in Ohio's economic growth. In 1959, the St. Lawrence Seaway

The Willys-Overland Motor Company in Toledo made the Jeeps used in World War II.

During the 1950s and 1960s, many people chose to live in suburbs like this one outside Dayton.

opened. The seaway connected the Great Lakes with the Atlantic Ocean. Cities such as Ashtabula, Cleveland, and Toledo became ports that could ship Ohio products overseas.

Automobiles continued to reshape society. By the mid-1950s, most Ohio families owned at least one car. The increased number of cars called for more paved roads. The Ohio Turnpike opened in 1955. Cars enabled workers to live farther away from their jobs in cities. Many middle-class white Ohioans moved to suburbs outside the central cities. About 170,000 whites moved out of Cleveland's city limits to such communities as Rocky River and Shaker Heights. Meanwhile, more blacks moved into Ohio's cities. About 100,000 African Americans moved to Cleveland from southern states in the 1950s and 1960s.

THE STRUGGLE FOR CIVIL RIGHTS

Many African Americans in Ohio's cities were crowded into run-down neighborhoods where crime was rampant. Blacks faced **discrimination** in jobs, education, and housing. Ernest J. Waits Sr., Cincinnati's first black disc jockey, told of a second-grade teacher not allowing him to share a textbook with a white student: "They made a civil rights fighter out of me that day."

Frustrated with being treated as second-class citizens, African Americans organized a nationwide struggle for equal rights in the 1960s. While most of these protests were peaceful, cities such as Cleveland and Dayton erupted in riots. African Americans and some whites worked to ensure voting rights for all citizens and to end racial discrimination. In 1967, Cleveland voters elected Carl Burton Stokes the first black mayor of a major American city.

In the 1960s, Ohioans also struggled with issues involving the Vietnam War. Students held antiwar demonstrations on college campuses all over the state. The most serious confrontation occurred at Kent State University in May 1970, when Ohio National Guard troops fired into a crowd of war protesters, killing four students and wounding nine others.

MINI-BIO

CARL BURTON STOKES: BREAKING BARRIERS

Carl Burton Stokes (1927–1996) was Cleveland's first African American mayor. He grew up in a federal housing project for low-income families in Cleveland. He became a lawyer and in 1962 was elected state representative. As mayor, he asked blacks and whites to join together in solving Cleveland's problems. He opened city jobs to African Americans and to women. He later became the country's first African American television news anchor and went on to serve as a judge and an ambassador. A federal courthouse in Cleveland is named after him.

 Want to know more? See www.ohiohistorycentral.org/entry.php?rec=1849

WORD TO KNOW

discrimination *unequal treatment based on race, gender, religion, or other factors*

MINI-BIO

GLORIA STEINEM: CHAMPION OF WOMEN'S RIGHTS

The granddaughter of an early suffragette who fought for women's right to vote, Gloria Steinem (1934–) carried on the family tradition and became a leader of the modern women's movement. Born in Toledo, she became interested in journalism and politics while in college. She helped found the National Women's Political Caucus in 1971 and cofounded Ms. Magazine in 1972. Steinem was inducted into the National Women's Hall of Fame in 1993, and today she continues to lecture and write books.

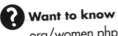 **Want to know more?** See www.greatwomen. org/women.php?action=viewone&id=150

WOMEN'S RIGHTS

Women enjoyed good job opportunities for a brief time during World War II, but once male soldiers returned home, those opportunities vanished. In the 1960s and 1970s, a women's movement emerged in Ohio and all over the United States. Women demanded equal treatment in housing, jobs, and education. They had many notable successes. In 1955, women earned only 64 cents to every dollar earned by a man. By 2005, they earned 77 cents for every dollar earned by a man.

Women also helped win passage in 1972 of Title IX, a federal law that bans discrimination in education, including school athletics. It enabled more female students in Ohio's high schools and colleges to participate in sports.

OHIO TODAY

By the 1970s, Ohio's big steel mills faced stiff competition from mills in other countries and were hampered by old equipment. In addition, the price of the fuels that powered the mills rose. Many big Ohio steel mills laid off workers, and some shut down. As many Ohioans left for better opportunities in Florida, Arizona, and other Sunbelt states, Cleveland, Toledo, and other big Ohio cities joined what was called the Rust Belt. Old, decaying mills and factories dotted the landscape.

Many people stayed in Ohio and worked on solving the state's problems. Service industries—such as banking, finance, insurance, and real estate—grew, providing many new jobs in the state. Cleveland became one of the world's leading medical centers. Some Ohio workers were still able to find manufacturing jobs. A new Jeep plant opened in Toledo in 2001. Honda set up four new plants in Ohio. Making high-tech medical equipment became a growing business around Columbus.

Some older industries adjusted their operations. Workers and management learned to work together to make factories more efficient. Linda Straub, a union official at Acklin Stamping Company in Toledo, summed up the feeling of many Ohio workers: "The biggest thing that I think we have going for us right now is the attitude and the commitment to make it."

In the 21st century, Cincinnati and other Ohio cities are busy, vibrant centers of business.

READ ABOUT

Music students at
Oberlin College

CHAPTER SIX

PEOPLE

★

I N APRIL 2004, THE CLEVELAND *PLAIN DEALER* RAN AN ARTICLE ABOUT U.S. POET LAUREATE AND AKRON NATIVE RITA DOVE. Although she now lives in Virginia, Dove told the reporter that her outlook "has its feet on the ground but at the same time is looking around with that kind of pioneer spirit. . . . When I envision a backyard, it's going to be a Midwestern back yard, it's going to be an Akron back yard."

A view of an Amish farm in Ohio

PEOPLE FROM MANY LANDS

As poet laureate, Dove discovered "that there were people all over the country who . . . were eager to embrace the multitude of voices that can be heard through poetry . . . and that these different voices . . . embraced the richness of the country." Ohio is a state that reflects the diversity of the whole country. You might meet an apple grower near Marietta whose ancestors came from England or a German American woodworker from Parma whose ancestors arrived in the early 1800s. You might see African American and Irish American teenagers planning a Cleveland Heights block party, an Indian chef cooking a large pot of spicy black lentils for her

Poet laureate Rita Dove

Columbus restaurant, children performing Hungarian folk dances in Dayton, or a young Puerto Rican Catholic couple worshipping at a Spanish language service in a Cleveland church.

Ohio's largest ethnic groups trace their roots to Germany, England, and Ireland. People of German descent make up about 25 percent of Ohio's population. In 1839, German immigrants established Cleveland's Jewish community. People of English and Irish ancestry account for almost 21 percent of Ohioans. Ohio also has large groups of Hungarians and Russians. Nearly 12 percent of Ohioans are African American.

An estimated 40,000 Old Order Amish live in Ohio, mostly in the east-central part of the state. The Amish are a religious group who believe in living simply. They do not own tractors, cars, or electric appliances. They are farmers and craftspeople who make especially fine quilts and furniture.

CITY, SUBURB, AND COUNTRY

More than 11 million people call Ohio home, and more than 9.2 million of them live in and around Ohio's biggest cities. The three largest **metropolitan areas** are Cincinnati-Middletown, Cleveland-Elyria-Mentor, and Columbus. Most rural communities are near metropolitan areas.

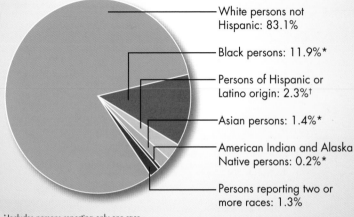

People QuickFacts

White persons not Hispanic: 83.1%

Black persons: 11.9%*

Persons of Hispanic or Latino origin: 2.3%†

Asian persons: 1.4%*

American Indian and Alaska Native persons: 0.2%*

Persons reporting two or more races: 1.3%

* Includes persons reporting only one race
† Hispanics may be of any race, so they also are included in applicable race categories
Source: U.S. Census Bureau, 2005 estimate

WORD TO KNOW

metropolitan areas *cities and all the suburbs surrounding them*

Ohio Population Growth

This chart shows Ohio's population growth between 1800 and 2000, and it projects that by 2010 there will be more than 11.5 million people living in the state.

Source: U.S. Census Bureau

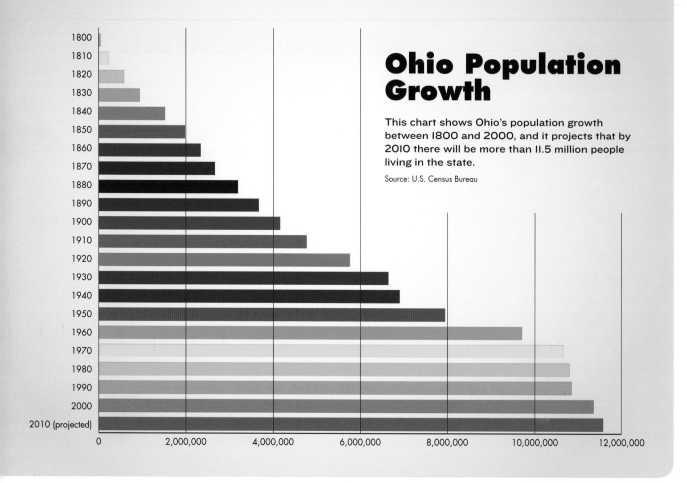

Big City Life

This list shows the population of Ohio's biggest cities.

Columbus 733,203
Cleveland 444,313
Cincinnati 332,252
Toledo 298,446
Akron 209,704

Source: U.S. Census Bureau, 2006 estimate

All of Ohio's cities except for Columbus (which has expanded its borders to include many suburbs) have lost population since the 1970s as people moved to the suburbs. At the same time, the population in suburbs has grown. And the population of the whole state increased by almost 5 percent from 1990 to 2000 as people moved in from other areas and other countries.

Many Ohioans live in the suburbs, but some live in houses or apartment buildings in the cities. Some also live on farms or in rural areas. In 2000, about 34 percent of Ohioans lived in small towns or townships, places beyond the suburbs but not entirely rural.

Where Ohioans Live

The colors on this map indicate population density throughout the state.
The darker the color, the more people live there.

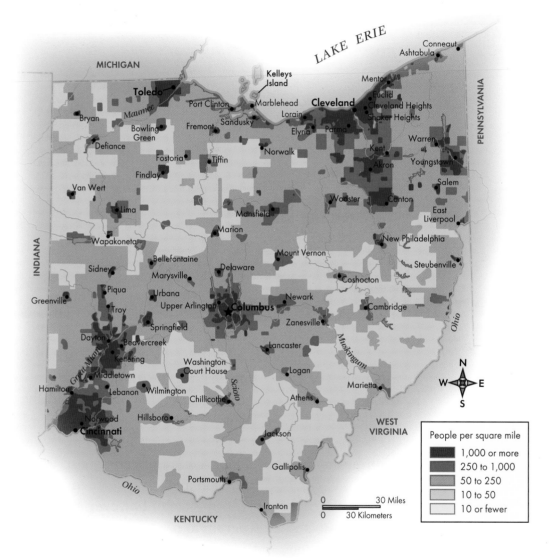

People per square mile

	1,000 or more
	250 to 1,000
	50 to 250
	10 to 50
	10 or fewer

GOING TO SCHOOL

Ohio has more than 4,400 schools for children from kindergarten through high school. Most of Ohio's schools are public. Churches and other private groups run about 860 private schools. Ohio has more than 260 community

Math students at a Toledo school

schools, also known as charter schools. Charter schools are privately run, profit-making institutions that students can go to for free because they are funded by public money and private donations.

Some public and community high schools focus on training students for a job. A student can choose from 16 types of careers, from food and agriculture to health sciences. Most schools in the state, however, follow a college preparatory program to prepare students to get a college degree.

Students who want to attend public college can choose from 13 state universities with 24 branches. The flagship university is Ohio State University. For students who want to study close to home, there are 15 community colleges throughout the state.

Ohio also has several top-ranked private colleges and universities. Case Western Reserve University in Cleveland attracts researchers as well as students from all over the world. Oberlin College in Oberlin was the first American college to give degrees to women and African Americans. Founded in 1824, Kenyon College in Gambier is the oldest private institution of higher learning in Ohio.

WRITERS AND POETS

Ohio writers have produced several American classics. Toni Morrison received a Pulitzer Prize for Fiction in 1988 for her novel *Beloved*. In 1993, Morrison was awarded the Nobel Prize in Literature. In the early 1900s, Zane Grey, a native of Zanesville, wrote more than 60 novels telling tales of the Wild West. Sherwood Anderson, born in Camden, was an early 20th-century novelist who set his classic book, *Winesburg, Ohio*, in a fictitious Ohio town. Earl Derr Biggers, born in Warren in 1884, created the Chinese American detective Charlie Chan. Virginia Hamilton, a children's book writer, won every major award for children's book writing before she died in 2002.

Paul Laurence Dunbar of Dayton was one of the greatest poets of the early 1900s. James Wright grew up during the Depression. His poems bring to life those grim times for Ohio's industrial workers and their families. Rita Dove, born in Akron in

MINI-BIO

TONI MORRISON: OUTSTANDING STORYTELLER

Novelist Toni Morrison (1932–), born in Lorain, was the first African American to win a Nobel Prize. In 1993, she was awarded the prize in literature for her powerful stories about African American experiences and feelings. She grew up in a working-class family that loved storytelling. Her novel *Beloved*, about a former enslaved woman, won a Pulitzer Prize in 1988. Morrison continues to write and teach.

? Want to know more? See http://nobelprize.org/nobel_prizes/literature/laureates/1993/morrison-bio.html

1952, won a Pulitzer Prize for her work, some of which deals with African American themes. Nikki Giovanni, who grew up in a suburb of Cincinnati, became an award-winning poet whose works were inspired by the civil rights movement.

Some very witty writers were born in Ohio. Humorist James G. Thurber was born in Columbus in 1894. He wrote funny stories and drew cartoons for *The New Yorker* magazine. Another humorist, Erma Bombeck, was born in Dayton. She made millions of people laugh with her stories about everyday life printed in newspapers around the country every week and in her many books.

THE MUSIC SCENE

Ohio's Cleveland Orchestra is one of the world's greatest orchestras. The Cincinnati Pops delivers classical music with a lighter touch. Both orchestras make recordings on Cleveland's Telarc label. Kathleen Battle, a great opera singer, was born in Portsmouth in 1948.

Several 20th-century music and movie stars came out of Ohio, including Dean Martin and Doris Day. Hailing from Middletown, the McGuire Sisters were a hugely popular singing trio in the 1940s and 1950s. The four Mills Brothers, American jazz and pop singers, were all born in Piqua in the 1910s.

MINI-BIO

ROY ROGERS: KING OF THE COWBOYS

A favorite cowboy hero of millions of American kids, Roy Rogers (1911–1998) was born in Cincinnati. His real name was Leonard Franklin Slye. He learned to ride horses and play the guitar on his family's farm near Portsmouth. In 1930, he moved to California and became a country-western musician and movie star. Rogers, his wife, Dale Evans, and his horse, Trigger, made about 100 movies and starred in a television show. The Roy Rogers restaurant chain is named for him.

? Want to know more? See www. ohiohistorycentral.org/entry.php?rec=1807

Drew Carey (left) in a scene from *The Drew Carey Show*, **which was set in Cleveland**

ACTORS AND COMICS

Some of America's best-known comedians came from Cleveland. Although Bob Hope was born in England, his family moved to Cleveland in 1907, when he was a young boy. He gave some of his first performances in Cleveland. Drew Carey was born in Cleveland, and his sitcom, *The Drew Carey Show*, which aired from 1995 to 2004, was set in Cleveland. Another Clevelander, Arsenio Hall, rose to fame in the 1990s as a comedian, actor, and talk-show host.

MINI-BIO

MARTIN SHEEN: MOVIE AND TELEVISION SUPERSTAR

Few people would recognize the name Ramón Gerardo Antonio Estévez (1940–) as one of America's biggest TV and movie stars. We know this celebrity of mixed Spanish and Irish descent as Martin Sheen. Born in Dayton, he went on to star in films such as *Apocalypse Now* (1979) and *Catch Me If You Can* (2002). He also played the U.S. president in the TV series *The West Wing*.

❓ Want to know more? See www.pbs.org/kcet/globaltribe/voices/voi_sheen.html

80

LARRY DOBY: BASEBALL GREAT

As an outfielder for the Cleveland Indians, Larry Doby (1923–2003) became the first African American player in the American League. In the 1940s, when Major League teams refused to hire African Americans, he was an All-Star second baseman in the Negro Leagues. Then, in 1947, the Indians hired him. He was inducted to the National Baseball Hall of Fame in 1998.

Want to know more? See www.baseballhalloffame.org/hofers/detail.jsp?playerId=113411

OHIO SPORTS

Ohio sports fans have plenty of teams to cheer for. Ohio boasts two Major League Baseball teams, two professional football teams, and two professional basketball teams. Fans pile into Cleveland's Jacobs Field hoping the Cleveland Indians will win their division and play in the World Series as they did in the late 1990s.

A young fan outside Jacobs Field, home of the Cleveland Indians

An excited crowd gets ready to watch the Cleveland Cavaliers in the first game of the 2007 NBA Finals.

The Cincinnati Bengals and the Cleveland Browns provide Ohio's pro football action. The Bengals played in the Super Bowl twice during the 1980s. Ohio's basketball fans root for the Cleveland Cavaliers. They also cheer on the Cleveland Rockers, Ohio's Women's National Basketball Association team.

Men's and women's college sports are also popular in Ohio. The Ohio State University football team has played for the national championship three times since 2000. The university is especially proud of its women's basketball team, which has produced stars such as forward Katie Smith and center Jessica Davenport, who were picked for professional teams in the Women's National Basketball Association.

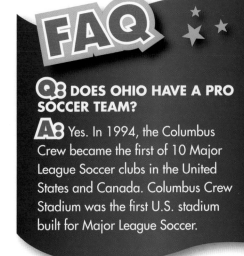

FAQ

Q8 DOES OHIO HAVE A PRO SOCCER TEAM?

A8 Yes. In 1994, the Columbus Crew became the first of 10 Major League Soccer clubs in the United States and Canada. Columbus Crew Stadium was the first U.S. stadium built for Major League Soccer.

Are you superstitious? Some Ohioans carry a buckeye nut to bring them good luck.

Candy buckeyes

HOW TO TALK LIKE AN OHIOAN

How do Ohioans talk? It depends on where you are in the state. Along the western part of the Ohio River, many Ohioans speak with a southern lilt. People in a certain city there might say they are from "Cincinnatah." Some people in the eastern part of Ohio have an Appalachian ring to the way they speak. When they talk about family, they probably say "kin."

A "buckeye" is someone who lives in Ohio. The nickname comes from the buckeye trees that once grew all over Ohio's plains. The Buckeyes, the Ohio State football team, play in the Horseshoe, the nickname for the U-shaped stadium.

HOW TO EAT LIKE AN OHIOAN

How about a buckeye? Say "no thanks" to a buckeye nut. Nuts from buckeye trees are poisonous to humans. But who could pass up a candy buckeye, a special Ohio sweet? These balls of peanut butter mixture are covered in chocolate. They look like buckeye nuts.

Ohioans enjoy the many kinds of foods grown in the Ohio Valley. They munch corn on the cob, scrambled eggs from Ohio chickens, and pop popcorn for an evening snack. Ohioans enjoy desserts made with the apples, peaches, and other fruits grown in Ohio.

Basket of peaches

Tomato juice

MENU

WHAT'S ON THE MENU IN OHIO?

Apple muffin

Tomato Juice

Tomato juice is the official state beverage of Ohio. An Ohio farmer in Reynoldsburg in 1870 introduced the tomato we know today.

Cincinnati Chili

Folks in Cincinnati like their chili served up with a portion of pasta.

Buckeye Burgers

You can find these special Ohio hamburgers at select restaurants in Ohio. The secret ingredients include coffee and brown sugar.

Apples

Ever since the days of Johnny Appleseed, who planted apple trees all over Ohio in the 1800s, Ohioans have loved apples and anything made with them, such as apple cake, apple crumb pie, apple muffins, and apple crisp.

Hungarian Goulash

Hungarian goulash is a hearty soup or stew made with beef and sometimes pork. Green or red peppers and lots of onions give it plenty of flavor. But the secret to Hungarian goulash is Hungarian paprika.

Cincinnati chili

TRY THIS RECIPE
Fried Cornmeal Mush

One food early Ohio settlers could count on for dinner was a bowl of cornmeal mush. Fried cornmeal mush is still a favorite dish in Ohio's Amish country and Appalachian region. Try this version and be sure to have a grown-up help.

Ingredients:
4 cups water
1 cup yellow cornmeal
1 teaspoon salt
1 teaspoon sugar
cooking spray and vegetable oil

Instructions:
1. Boil 3 cups of the water in a saucepan.
2. In a bowl, mix cornmeal, salt, and sugar.
3. Slowly add the remaining cup of water to the cornmeal mixture in the bowl while constantly stirring, until all the cornmeal is wet.
4. Slowly add the cornmeal mixture to the boiling water while stirring, until thick.
5. Cover and turn the heat to low. Cook for about 30 minutes, stirring every 5 minutes.
6. Coat a 13 inch x 9 inch cake pan with cooking spray and pour the cornmeal mixture into it. Let it cool.
7. Cover the cooled mixture with plastic wrap and set it in the refrigerator to chill.
8. Cut slices from the chilled cakelike mixture.
9. Heat a frying pan over medium heat; coat the bottom of the pan with vegetable oil.
10. Fry cornmeal slices in the pan until brown.
11. Serve with butter and syrup.

READ ABOUT

Students visiting
the statehouse
in Columbus

CHAPTER SEVEN

GOVERNMENT

★

O HIO'S FIRST CONSTITUTION, ADOPTED IN 1803, SET UP A WEAK GOVERNMENT. It called for three branches of government—legislative, executive, and judicial. The legislative branch, or General Assembly, was made up of a senate and a house of representatives. The first constitution gave most power to the lawmakers. The governor could not veto any bills passed by the General Assembly.

SEE IT HERE!

GHOST TOURS

On October evenings, the Ohio State-house hosts Ghost Tours. Costumed guides with oil lamps light the way through shadowed halls and passageways. Odd items are on display from the old Statehouse Relic Room, which once housed chess pieces carved from bones. Creepy!

WORD TO KNOW

veto *to reject a proposed law*

BECOMING MORE DEMOCRATIC

Ohio's second constitution was adopted in 1851. Under this constitution, the governor still did not have much authority or **veto** power, but now voters were allowed to elect judges and some state officials. Only adult white men could vote. The 1851 constitution has been amended many times to make it more democratic. In 1903, the governor finally gained veto power.

In 1912, a convention was held to modernize the 1851 constitution by adding amendments. One amendment allowed large cities "home rule," which is more control over their own affairs. Other amendments provided for the initiative, which allows citizens to propose laws; the referendum, which allows citizens to vote on

Capital City

This map shows places of interest in Columbus, Ohio's capital city.

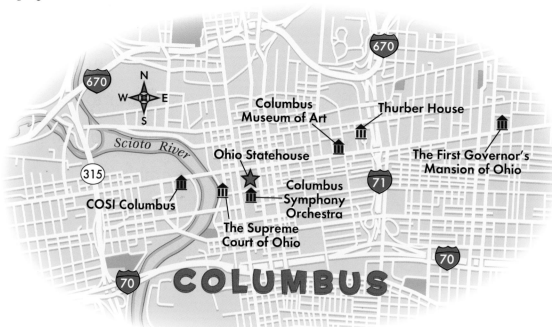

laws; and the recall, which allows citizens to vote elected officials out of office before their terms are completed.

WHERE IT HAPPENS

Most government action takes place in the state capitol, or statehouse, in Columbus. It's where the legislature meets and the governor's office is located. The Ohio Supreme Court and other judiciary offices are conveniently across the street from the statehouse.

Capitol Facts

Here are some fascinating facts about Ohio's state capitol.

Exterior height . . . . 158 feet (48 m)
Height of interior dome . . . . 125 feet (38 m)
Building area. . . . . .2 acres (0.8 ha)
Surrounding park . . . . 10 acres (4 ha)
Location . . . . .Capitol Square, Columbus
Construction dates 1839–1861
Cost of construction . . . .$1.3 million
($100 million in today's dollars)

The capitol in Columbus

Ohio State Government

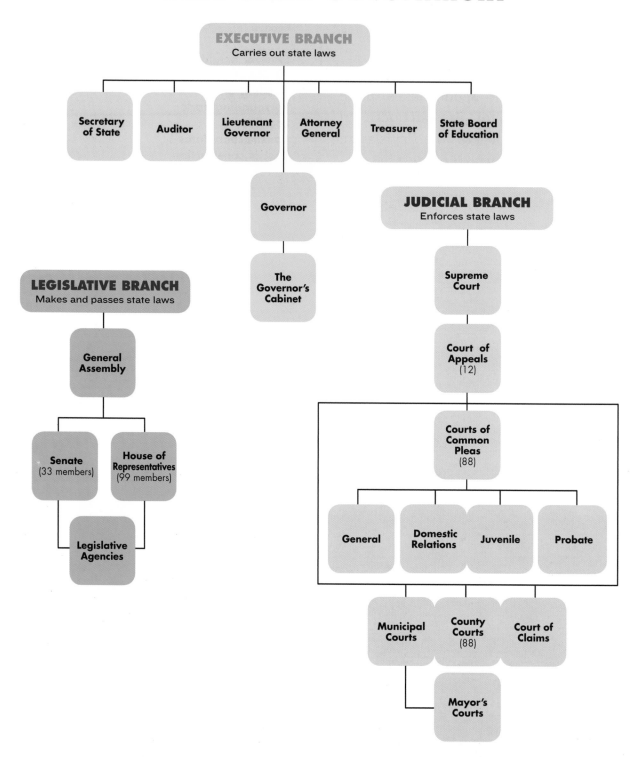

THINK ABOUT IT!

A Strong Executive

The authors of Ohio's first constitution did not want the executive branch to have much power. A strong governor could suspend the rule of law and become a tyrant or a dictator. So Ohioans gave more power to the legislators.

The founders of the United States had also feared a strong executive. They had won a revolution against rule by a tyrannical British king. "[T]he Constitution's framers . . . were revolutionaries who detested kings," said a 2007 *New York Times* editorial regarding presidential power in an age of terrorism, "and their great concern when they established the United States was that they not accidentally create a kingdom. To guard against it, they sharply limited presidential authority."

On the other hand, some people believe that in a democracy a strong chief executive is needed to provide stability, and that the right of the people to vote an executive out of office protects against **tyranny** and other abuses. The question of how much power to give to the executive became a major question after the terrorist attacks of September 11, 2001. Vice President Dick Cheney summed up his views in 2005: "I believe in a strong, robust executive authority. . . . In the day and age we live in, the nature of the threats we face, the president of the United States needs to have his constitutional powers unimpaired, if you will, in terms of the conduct of national security policy."

THE EXECUTIVE BRANCH

The governor is the head of Ohio's executive branch. The governor names the heads of 22 government agencies in charge of areas such as health, public safety, and natural resources. The legislature has to approve the governor's choices.

The lieutenant governor takes over if the governor can't work. The lieutenant governor can also lead an agency. The attorney general is Ohio's top lawyer. His

WORD TO KNOW

tyranny *a cruel and unfair use of power*

LOUIS STOKES: CONGRESSMAN

The first African American U.S. congressman from Ohio, Louis Stokes (1925–) was born in Cleveland. His brother, Carl B. Stokes, was the first African American mayor of Cleveland. After serving in the army during World War II, Louis Stokes became a lawyer. In 1968, he was elected to the U.S. House of Representatives.

? Want to know more? See bioguide.congress. gov/scripts/biodisplay.pl?index=S000948

WORD TO KNOW

sponsor *to propose or write a bill*

or her job is to protect consumers and support police in fighting crime. The office of the secretary of state is responsible for approving new businesses, heading voter registration, and overseeing all voting in the state. The auditor and the treasurer keep tabs on the state's money. The auditor is the state accountant, who makes sure that the state's money is being spent wisely—and legally. The treasurer is in charge of collecting all taxes and investing the money.

THE LEGISLATIVE BRANCH

The Ohio General Assembly is made up of a house of representatives and a senate. Either a senator or a representative can **sponsor** a bill, the first step toward passing a law. Each chamber amends and votes separately, which often results in two somewhat different bills on the same topic. To resolve the differences in the two bills, they are sent to a joint committee

Representing Ohioans

This list shows the number of elected officials who represent Ohio, both on the state and national levels.

OFFICE	NUMBER	LENGTH OF TERM
State senators	33	4 years
State representatives	99	2 years
U.S. senators	2	6 years
U.S. representatives	18	2 years
Presidential electors	20	—

Ohio Governor Bob Taft delivers his State of the State speech in the house of representatives chamber in January 2006.

to work out the final details. Once the joint committee comes up with a compromise bill, both the house and the senate must pass it and the governor must sign it in order for the bill to become law. If the governor vetoes the bill, a vote by a three-fifths majority of both houses can override a veto.

THE JUDICIAL BRANCH

Ohio has three levels of state courts, which hear criminal cases, involving broken laws, or civil cases, involving lawsuits. The lowest level is the common pleas court, one for

WEIRD AND WACKY LAWS

The state of Ohio is concerned about the treatment of animals. This is a good thing. Nevertheless, some animal laws in Ohio are just downright strange. Take a look at these examples:

- Anyone who wants to keep a bear as a pet must get a license.
- No whale hunting is allowed on Sundays.
- If you own a tiger and it escapes, you must tell the police within one hour.
- People in Cleveland must get a hunting license to catch mice.
- If you throw a snake at someone in Toledo, you are breaking the law.
- Police officers in Paulding can quiet a noisy dog by biting it.

SALMON P. CHASE: ANTISLAVERY LAWYER

As an attorney, Salmon P. Chase (1808–1873) helped so many runaway slaves in court that he was called the "attorney general of the fugitive slaves." When a mob ripped apart the office of an antislavery newspaper publisher and threw his printing press into the river, the Cincinnati mayor watched approvingly, and no police appeared. Then the mob set out to find the publisher and lynch him. A young, broad-shouldered Chase stopped them and drove them off. He went on to serve as a U.S. senator, Ohio governor, U.S. secretary of the treasury, and chief justice of the U.S. Supreme Court.

? Want to know more? See www.ohiohistorycentral. org/entry.php?rec=92

Ohio is called a barometer state. It has nothing to do with the weather. Ohio has such a diverse population that politicians think of it as a place to test how Americans as a whole feel about candidates and issues.

each county. Someone who is convicted of a crime or loses a lawsuit in a common pleas court can go to Ohio's courts of appeals. Decisions by a court of appeals can be appealed to Ohio's supreme court, the highest court in the state. It is made up of a chief justice and seven other justices, who are elected to six-year terms.

COUNTIES, CITIES, AND VILLAGES

Local governments provide services such as police and fire protection, public health, and building inspection. They also collect property taxes to pay for these services. State law requires counties to be governed by a three-member commission, unless a county votes to become a charter county, which can decide what form of government it wants. The only charter county in Ohio is Summit County. It has an elected executive and a seven-member council.

By Ohio law, a city must have at least 5,000 residents. A community with fewer people than that is a village. Most Ohio cities have a mayor and a city council. Others are governed by commissions or by a council and a city manager. On the local level, Ohio has county courts, municipal courts, and specialized courts that deal with wills or crimes committed by young people.

Ohio Counties

This map shows the 88 counties in Ohio. Columbus, the state capital, is indicated with a star.

MICHIGAN

LAKE ERIE

Toledo

Cleveland

WILLIAMS | FULTON | LUCAS | LAKE | ASHTABULA

OTTAWA | GEAUGA

CUYAHOGA

DEFIANCE | HENRY | WOOD | SANDUSKY | ERIE | TRUMBULL

LORAIN

PAULDING | SENECA | HURON | MEDINA | SUMMIT | PORTAGE

PUTNAM | MAHONING

HANCOCK

VAN WERT | CRAWFORD | ASHLAND | STARK | COLUMBIANA

WYANDOT | WAYNE

ALLEN | RICHLAND

HARDIN | CARROLL

MERCER | AUGLAIZE | MARION | HOLMES

MORROW | JEFFERSON

LOGAN | KNOX | TUSCARAWAS

SHELBY | UNION | COSHOCTON | HARRISON

DELAWARE

DARKE | CHAMPAIGN | LICKING

MIAMI | GUERNSEY | BELMONT

Columbus

CLARK | MADISON | FRANKLIN | MUSKINGUM

MONTGOMERY | FAIRFIELD | NOBLE | MONROE

PREBLE | GREENE | PERRY | MORGAN

PICKAWAY

FAYETTE

BUTLER | WARREN | HOCKING | WASHINGTON

CLINTON | ROSS | ATHENS

HAMILTON | VINTON

Cincinnati | HIGHLAND | MEIGS

CLERMONT | PIKE

JACKSON

BROWN | GALLIA

ADAMS | SCIOTO

Ohio

LAWRENCE

KENTUCKY

INDIANA

PENNSYLVANIA

WEST VIRGINIA

Ohio

N
W E
S

0 — 30 Miles
0 — 30 Kilometers

County boundary

MAKING DEMOCRACY WORK

Democratic government needs more than government officials to function well. It also needs active citizens and civic organizations. In Ohio, the three branches of government and teenagers are working together

MINI-BIO

VICTORIA CLAFLIN WOODHULL: PRESIDENTIAL CANDIDATE

In 1872, Victoria Claflin Woodhull (1838–1927), a native of Homer, became the first woman to run for president. At age 15, she married. Ten years later, she divorced and moved to New York City with her sister. Wealthy businessman Cornelius Vanderbilt gave the sisters money to start a stock brokerage. The sisters also founded a magazine that promoted women's rights.

? Want to know more? See www. ohiohistorycentral.org/entry.php?rec=420

A lawyer speaks with his client in one of Ohio's juvenile courts.

WORD TO KNOW

juvenile *referring to young people*

to help other teens become responsible drivers. The legislative branch has passed traffic laws such as speed limits. The executive branch enforces these laws. With its siren wailing, a police car pulls a teenage driver over for speeding. Then the judicial branch comes in. The teen goes to court. If the teenager is a first-time offender, the judge can order the youth to attend a safety education program twice a month.

The program, called CARTEEN, was the idea of Ohio youth groups and the Ohio State University Extension. They involved county **juvenile** courts and the State Highway Patrol, whose officers help teens teach the courses. Since the program began in 1987, the number of teens arrested twice for traffic violations has dropped by almost 90 percent. That's democracy at work!

OHIO PRESIDENTS

William Henry Harrison (1773–1841), ninth president of the United States (1841), was born in Virginia but was living near Cincinnati when he was elected. After serving only one month, he died of pneumonia.

Ulysses S. Grant (1822–1885) was America's 18th president (1869–1877). As a Civil War general, he became head of the Union army that defeated Confederate forces. But his presidency could not solve the problems of Reconstruction (the rebuilding of the South after the war).

Rutherford B. Hayes (1822–1893), the 19th U.S. president (1877–1881), ended Reconstruction by withdrawing federal troops from the South.

James A. Garfield (1831–1881), the 20th president of the United States (1881), served only four months before he died in office. A man who had been denied a political job shot and killed him. Garfield's death inspired Congress to create the civil service system. Under this system, most jobs in the federal government are given out based on people's qualifications rather than whether they support the president.

Benjamin Harrison (1833–1901), the grandson of President William Henry Harrison, was the 23rd president of the United States (1889–1893). He lost his bid for reelection to Grover Cleveland.

William McKinley (1843–1901), the 25th president (1897–1901), declared war on Spain after the U.S. battleship *Maine* mysteriously exploded in the harbor at Havana, Cuba. The United States won the Spanish-American War and gained Guam, Puerto Rico, and the Philippines. McKinley was assassinated during his second term.

William Howard Taft (1857–1930), the 27th president (1909–1913), did not want to be president; he wanted to be a Supreme Court justice. His dream came true in 1921, when he was appointed chief justice of the U.S. Supreme Court.

Warren G. Harding (1865–1923), the 29th president (1921–1923), is remembered for the scandals that troubled his administration. He died in office.

Ulysses S. Grant

William Howard Taft

Q: WHY IS OHIO CALLED THE MOTHER OF PRESIDENTS?

A: Eight U.S. presidents had Ohio roots. Seven were actually born in Ohio, and one—William Henry Harrison—centered his political career in the state.

State Flag

The Ohio flag's triangle shapes represent the state's hills and valleys, and the stripes represent its roads and waterways. The 17 stars stand for the 13 original states, plus the four that were added to make Ohio the 17th state admitted into the Union. The white circle with its red center is a buckeye, for the Buckeye State. By itself, the white circle also makes an O for "Ohio." The Ohio legislature adopted the official flag in 1902.

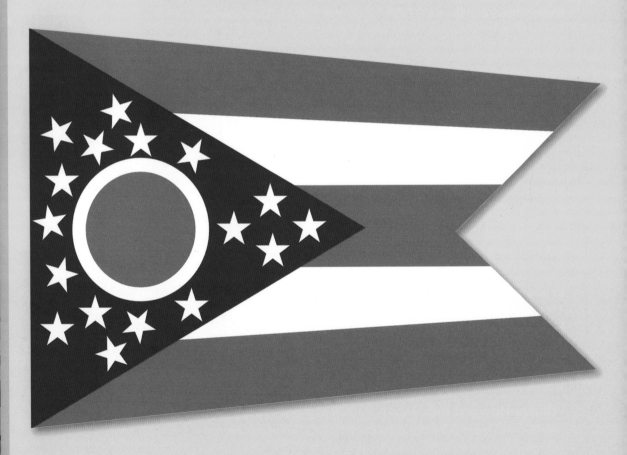

State Seal

The seal is a picture of a typical Ohio wheat field by the Scioto River, with Mount Logan in the background. The sheaf of wheat on the harvested field represents the importance of agriculture in Ohio's history. The 17 arrows standing next to it represent both Ohio's Indians and its place as the 17th state. Thirteen rays shine out from the sun, representing the 13 colonies. The seal has been updated over the course of 150 years. In earlier versions, a canal boat floated on the river. The current state seal became official in 1996.

READ ABOUT

Jeep Wrangler
chassis being
assembled at
an automotive
plant in Toledo

ECONOMY

★

NEXT TIME YOU RIDE IN THE FAMILY CAR, THINK ABOUT THIS: WHERE DID THE PARTS THAT MAKE UP THE CAR COME FROM? There is a good chance that a number of its parts were made in Ohio, and that the entire vehicle was assembled there, too. Ohio is one of the leading makers of automobile parts. Ohio remains the nation's third-leading manufacturing state. Manufacturing is big in the cities. In the countryside, agriculture is king. Nevertheless, the service industry is now at the top of Ohio's economy.

An information-technology specialist helps students scan their computers for viruses.

MINI-BIO

GRANVILLE T. WOODS, GREAT INVENTOR

The many inventions of Granville T. Woods (1856–1910) greatly improved safety on railroad trains. He was born in Columbus and opened a machine shop in Cincinnati. He invented overhead power lines for electric railroads and a way for moving trains to send messages to control towers. He had patents on more than 60 inventions. People often compared him with another Ohio-born inventor, Thomas Edison.

? **Want to know more?** See www. ohiohistorycentral.org/entry.php?rec=421

SERVICE WITH A SMILE

All kinds of services are provided by Ohioans. The person who installs your cable TV hookup, the pizza delivery person, your teacher, and your doctor all work in the service industry. People who issue insurance, work in banks, and sell houses are also service industry workers. Since the 1970s, service industries have overtaken manufacturing as the biggest part of Ohio's economy.

Several major companies are headquartered in Ohio. They include Fifth Third Bancorp, Progressive Insurance, Nationwide Insurance Enterprise, and American Financial Group. High-tech industries are also important. About 60,000 Ohioans work in the computer services industry. Some high-tech companies provide information. One of the biggest is the information company LexisNexis in Dayton. LexisNexis Web servers hold 5 billion documents with information about law, business, government, news, and just about anything else you can think of. Growth of Ohio's service industries is a good example of how the state is changing to keep up with the times.

MANUFACTURING INDUSTRY

Of all the goods made in Ohio, transportation equipment is the top moneymaker. Honda of America operates four Ohio plants. The plants turn out motorcycles, car engines, **transmissions**, and other parts. Workers at a Chrysler plant in Toledo build Jeep Liberties. Robots on a state-of-the-art production line in Springfield weld together truck cabs. Plants in Defiance, Stryker, and Paulding make parts for General Motors and Ford.

WORD TO KNOW

transmissions *mechanisms for transmitting power from a motor vehicle's engine to its wheels*

Top Products

Agriculture Beef cattle, corn, greenhouse and nursery products, hogs, milk, poultry products, soybeans

Manufacturing Chemicals, fabricated metal products, machinery, plastic and rubber products, primary metals, processed foods

Mining Coal, limestone, natural gas, salt, sandstone

A worker cuts up slabs of steel at International Steel Group, Inc., in Cleveland.

MINI-BIO

CHARLES F. KETTERING: AUTO WIZARD

Born on a farm near Loudonville, Charles F. Kettering (1876–1958) revolutionized automobiles. The first cars had to be started with a hand crank that was very difficult and dangerous. Working for Delco and General Motors, Kettering invented the electric car starter, electric headlights, spark plugs, the automatic transmission, and four-wheel brakes. He also helped set up the Sloan-Kettering Institute for Cancer Research in New York City.

? Want to know more? See www.pbs.org/wgbh/amex/streamliners/peopleevents/p_kettering.html

Car parts need metal, and Ohio has been turning ore into metal since 1802. The state's first blast furnace near Youngstown began making iron that year. Equipment in Ohio steel mills today is a far cry from the early vats of red-hot metal. Mill owners have spent billions of dollars to modernize Ohio's steel industry. The new mills are cleaner and more efficient. They make new types of stronger, lighter steel. Ohio is still the leading U.S. maker of steel.

The detergent in your washer and the paint on the living room walls may have come from Ohio. Chemicals of all kinds are made in Ohio. Cincinnati is the home of the giant manufacturer Procter & Gamble. The company's Ivorydale soap factory near Cincinnati is the biggest soap plant in the world. Sherwin-Williams Company, based in Cleveland, is the largest paint and coatings maker in the United States, and the second largest in the world. Ohio is also number one in rubber and plastics. More than 73,000 Ohioans work in these industries.

More than 62,000 Ohioans are busy making up some of your favorite foods. Auglaize County is the spot for milk products. Dannon has the world's largest yogurt

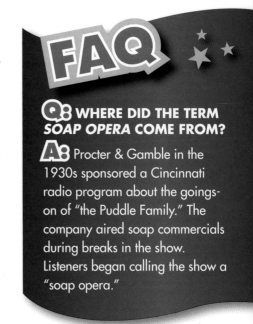

FAQ

Q8 WHERE DID THE TERM *SOAP OPERA* COME FROM?

A8 Procter & Gamble in the 1930s sponsored a Cincinnati radio program about the goings-on of "the Puddle Family." The company aired soap commercials during breaks in the show. Listeners began calling the show a "soap opera."

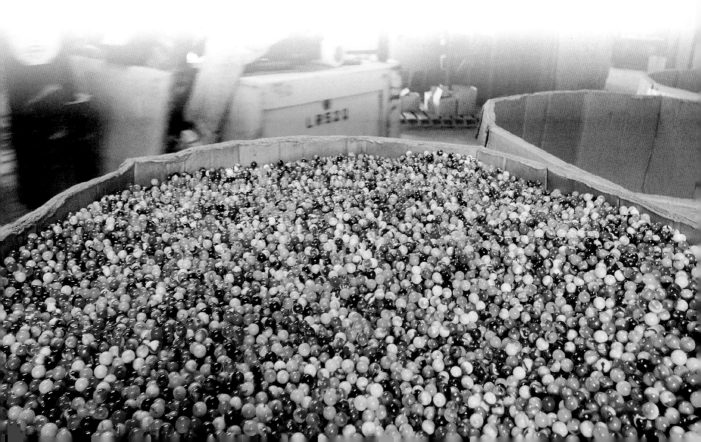

A container full of Dave's Classic collectible marbles at the Jabo, Inc., marble factory in Reno

This machine is filling plastic jugs with apple cider at a company in Pike Township.

SEE IT HERE!

A CAROUSEL FACTORY

Ohio factories build cars and trucks, which take you places. One factory builds something that takes you around in circles. The name of the company is Carousel Magic. Located in Mansfield, it builds carousels, or merry-go-rounds. On a tour of the factory, you can learn a lot about carousels. Skilled wood-carvers create horses, dragons, and other figures for riders. Painters color the figures with bright designs. Tour guides explain everything you might want to know about the history of these popular amusement park attractions.

factory there. Dairy Farm Products makes cottage cheese, ice cream, and other good things. These companies use 40 million pounds of milk a year. That's like having 25,000 cows working overtime every day.

Factories throughout Ohio turn out frozen foods, pet foods, ketchup, salad dressings, cookies, crackers, and soft drinks. Campbell's runs the world's largest soup factory in Napoleon. Bob Evans, The J. M. Smucker Company, Kroger, and Wendy's International are some big food companies headquartered in Ohio.

FARM PRODUCE

A drive through the rolling hills of Ohio's countryside takes you to farm country. You

Major Agricultural and Mining Products

This map shows where Ohio's major agricultural and mining products come from. See a cow? That means cattle are found there.

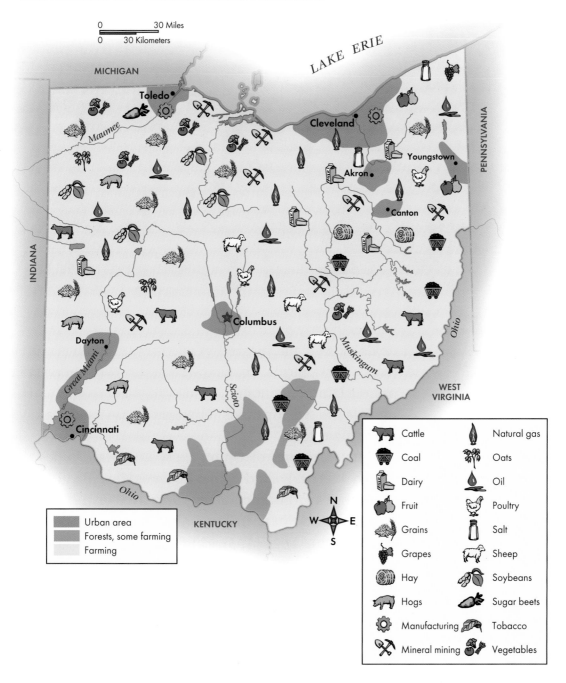

0   30 Miles
0   30 Kilometers

MICHIGAN

LAKE ERIE

Toledo

Maumee

Cleveland

Youngstown

Akron

PENNSYLVANIA

Canton

INDIANA

Columbus

Dayton

Great Miami

Ohio

Scioto

Muskingum

Ohio

WEST VIRGINIA

Cincinnati

KENTUCKY

N
W   E
S

	Urban area
	Forests, some farming
	Farming

Cattle		Natural gas	
Coal		Oats	
Dairy		Oil	
Fruit		Poultry	
Grains		Salt	
Grapes		Sheep	
Hay		Soybeans	
Hogs		Sugar beets	
Manufacturing		Tobacco	
Mineral mining		Vegetables	

Tomatoes tumble from a conveyor after passing through a harvester near Pemberville.

Ohio is the nation's top producer of greenhouse and nursery plants. Ohio grows more poinsettias than any other nursery plant.

will see plenty of farmhouses and barns surrounded by fields plowed and planted in neat rows. Ohio has more than 76,200 farms, making agriculture an important part of Ohio's economy. Fields of soybeans and corn provide the two top crops. These crops are used mainly to feed livestock.

Hogs are one of Ohio's most important types of livestock. The Poland China hog was developed from a number of different breeds in Ohio in the 1800s. Most pork and ham in the United States comes from Poland China hogs. Apples and peaches grow in Ohio orchards. Grapes and strawberries are also important fruit crops. Ohio is the third-largest producer of tomatoes. Ohio farmers also grow cucumbers, potatoes, and other kinds of vegetables.

COAL AND GAS

A drive through the rugged hills of Ohio's Appalachian region takes you to coal mining country. Mines may be deep underground or on the surface. Coal is still important to Ohio's economy. However, the amount of coal mined has dropped by about 50 percent. Some 55 million tons came from Ohio coal mines in 1970. Miners hauled out only about 22 million tons at the beginning of the 2000s. One reason for the drop is that Ohio coal does not burn very cleanly. Burning Ohio coal in factories and in plants to make electricity causes air pollution. New types of furnaces can burn coal more cleanly. Ohio miners hope that this "clean-coal technology" can help coal make a comeback. Natural gas and oil are other natural resources that come from the ground in Ohio. In addition, Ohio sandstone quarries lead the nation in the production of this building stone.

What Do Ohioans Do?

This color-coded chart shows what industries Ohioans work in.

- **21.6%** Educational services, health care, and social assistance, 1,146,539
- **17.3%** Manufacturing, 922,821
- **11.7%** Retail trade, 621,501
- **8.5%** Arts, entertainment, recreation, accommodation, and food services, 453,743

- **8.2%** Professional, scientific, management, administrative, and waste management services, 438,737
- **6.8%** Finance, insurance, real estate, rental, and leasing, 360,669
- **6.0%** Construction, 321,576
- **5.0%** Transportation, warehousing, and utilities, 264,005

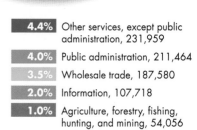

- **4.4%** Other services, except public administration, 231,959
- **4.0%** Public administration, 211,464
- **3.5%** Wholesale trade, 187,580
- **2.0%** Information, 107,718
- **1.0%** Agriculture, forestry, fishing, hunting, and mining, 54,056

Source: U.S. Census Bureau, 2005 estimate

CANADA

LAKE ERIE

MICHIGAN

Conneaut
Ashtabula
Geneva
Mentor
Cleveland Heights
Euclid
Cleveland
Shaker Heights

PENNSYLVANIA

Kelleys Island
Marblehead
Toledo
Port Clinton
Sandusky
Lorain
Fremont
Elyria
Parma
Milan
Norwalk
Kent
Warren
Archbold
Maumee
Defiance
Bowling Green
Fostoria
Tiffin
Findlay
Crawford
Shelby
Wooster
Youngstown

Van Wert
Lima
Mansfield
Lucas
Millersburg
Berlin
Canton
East Liverpool
New Philadelphia
Steubenville
Cadiz

Wapakoneta
Marion
Mount Vernon
Fort Recovery
Bellefontaine
Coshocton
Sidney
Marysville
Delaware
Geographic Center of Ohio
Greenville
West Liberty
Urbana
Cambridge
Piqua
Upper Arlington
Columbus
Newark
Greenwood
Troy
Springfield
Lancaster

INDIANA

Dayton
Beavercreek
Zanesville
Kettering
McConnelsville
Middletown
Lebanon
Wilmington
Logan
Marietta
Hamilton
Harrison
Chillicothe
Athens

WEST VIRGINIA

Norwood
Hillsboro
Cincinnati
Waverly
Jackson
Point Pleasant
Ohio
Scioto
Muskingum
Ohio
Gallipolis
Ripley
Portsmouth

KENTUCKY

Ironton

N
W   E
S

0   30 Miles
0   30 Kilometers

75 Interstate highway

CHAPTER NINE

TRAVEL GUIDE

★

D RIVING OHIO'S COUNTRY ROADS, YOU CAN WATCH THE SCENERY CHANGE FROM ROLLING HILLS TO RUGGED MOUNTAINS. There is water everywhere, from the shore of Lake Erie to the rivers that crisscross the state. From big-city excitement and historic monuments to Appalachian beauty and quiet, you'll find it in Ohio. Grab your map and let's take a tour.

← Follow along with this travel map. We'll begin in Archbold and end in Logan.

NORTH-WESTERN

THINGS TO DO: Tour an early 20th-century barbershop and a one-room schoolhouse, experience the Civil War through the eyes of a soldier, and enjoy thrills at an amusement park.

Archbold

★ **Sauder Village:** Here you'll learn how people lived in the early 1900s, when the Sauder Woodworking business was born. Costumed interpreters show how cabinets, wooden barrels, wool, quilts, and baskets were made. There is also a barbershop and a one-room schoolhouse.

Bowling Green

★ **American Civil War Museum of Ohio:** Dioramas show daily routines, medical care, and a pris-oner-of-war camp. You can try on clothes from Civil War days.

Lima

★ **Allen County Museum:** At this museum, you can see antique autos, a covered wagon, a World War II tank, and a steam locomo-tive, plus signal lanterns and other objects from the county's past.

SEE IT HERE!

KELLEYS ISLAND

This 4-square-mile (10 sq km) island in Lake Erie is a popular summer vacation spot. Tourists enjoy swimming, boating, hiking, fishing, and bird-watching. On the north side, the last retreating glacier carved a scar 400 feet (120 m) long and 35 feet (11 m) wide into the limestone.

Marblehead

★ **Marblehead Lighthouse:** On dark nights, the beacon from Marblehead Lighthouse kept sailors on Lake Erie from running into Ohio's rocky shore. The 1822 lighthouse is now the center of an Ohio state park.

Marblehead Lighthouse

African Safari Wildlife Park

Port Clinton

★ **African Safari Wildlife Park:** This 100-acre (40 ha) park is home to alpacas, camels, giraffes, zebras, and about 45 other animal species. You can feed the animals from a bucket of food supplied by the park.

Milan

★ **Thomas Edison's birthplace:** The simple redbrick house contains the type of furnishings the great inventor would have grown up with. Edison visited the house in 1923. Imagine how surprised he was to find it had no electricity!

WOW

Attractions have been luring thrill seekers to Cedar Point since the late 1800s. The first roller coaster was built there in 1892.

Sandusky

★ **Cedar Point Amusement Park:** With 17 roller coasters, the park calls itself the Roller Coaster Capital of the World.

Toledo

★ **Toledo Botanical Garden:** Here you can stroll the pathways through a variety of gardens, including the Shade Garden, the Aquatic Garden, the Perennial Garden, and the Grass Garden.

Wapakoneta

★ **Armstrong Air & Space Museum:** This museum houses the *Gemini 8* spacecraft, two of Neil Armstrong's space suits, and a moon rock. In simulators, you can experience what it feels like to land on the moon or be in space.

West Liberty

★ **Ohio Caverns:** Giant, teethlike formations fill Ohio's largest cave. Take a tour and find out how dripping water built the fantastic forms.

NORTH-EASTERN

THINGS TO DO: Take a tour through the Pro Football Hall of Fame and visit popcorn heaven.

Canton

★ **Hoover Historical Center:** Displays tell the story of the vacuum cleaner, which started when W. H. Hoover bought the rights to an odd-looking machine invented by janitor James Murray Spangler in the early 1900s.

SEE IT HERE!

PRO FOOTBALL HALL OF FAME

Learn all about the history of American football and the game's greatest players. You can view photos and memorabilia of players such as Gene Hickerson of the Cleveland Browns and Roger Staubach of the Dallas Cowboys.

Fans outside the Pro Football Hall of Fame

Cleveland

★ **A Christmas Story House:** Are you a fan of the classic holiday movie *A Christmas Story?* Brian Jones sure is. He bought and restored the house in which Ralphie and his family lived in the film. You can even buy a Leg Lamp.

★ **Maltz Museum of Jewish Heritage:** Celebrates the accomplishments of Cleveland's Jewish community through religious art and artifacts.

★ **Rock and Roll Hall of Fame and Museum:** This museum opened in Cleveland in 1995 to honor the great performers and the history of rock-and-roll music. It quickly became the city's number-one tourist attraction, bringing visitors and much-needed economic benefits to Cleveland. It displays items such as Chuck Berry's Gibson guitar and a shirt worn by Fats Domino. One exhibit explores the roots of rock and roll, while another looks at up-and-coming artists.

Chuck Berry's Gibson guitar

Crawford

★ **Crawford Auto-Aviation Museum:** The Panhard et Levassor was the first totally enclosed automobile. See this 1897 vehicle and 200 more antique autos and aircraft at the museum.

Lucas

★ **Malabar Farm State Park:** In the 1930s, environmentalist Louis Bromfield showed how sustainable farming methods could conserve soil on this farm. The visitor center teaches about recycling, alternative energy, and water conservation.

Marion

★ **Warren G. Harding Home:** See the home where the 29th president of the United States lived when he was elected in 1920. The 1891 Victorian house has been restored to look as it did in Harding's day.

★ **Wyandot Popcorn Museum:** This is the only museum in the world dedicated to popcorn. The collection includes antique popcorn machines and even a 1927 Ford popcorn truck!

Millersburg

★ **Amish Country Byway:** Watch out for horse-drawn buggies! This scenic Ohio road runs through the heart of Ohio's Amish country.

Berlin

★ **Amish & Mennonite Heritage Center:** At this site, you can enjoy Amish home cooking and shop for quilts, crafts, and other wares.

SOUTH-WESTERN

THINGS TO DO: Check out a great zoo, cheer on the Ohio State Buckeyes, or learn about historic earthworks.

SEE IT HERE!

CINCINNATI ZOO & BOTANICAL GARDEN

In 1872, caterpillars invaded Cincinnati. Fearful that they would eat every plant in town, concerned citizens brought 1,000 birds from Europe to eat the caterpillars. They kept the birds in a special house. The citizens gathered more animals and began to call themselves the Zoological Society of Cincinnati. The Cincinnati Zoo & Botanical Garden became one of the best zoos in the United States.

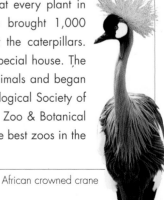

African crowned crane

Columbus

★ **The King Arts Complex:** Named in honor of Martin Luther King Jr., this facility is home to African American dance performances, jazz and gospel concerts, plays, and the Elijah Pierce Gallery.

★ **Ohio Statehouse:** See where Buckeyes make their laws and listen to legislators in session. You can learn about African American Ohioans in the George Washington Williams Room.

Ohio Stadium

★ **Ohio Stadium:** Built in 1922, this horseshoe-shaped football stadium is on the National Register of Historic Places. The Horseshoe is the home of the Ohio State Buckeyes football team and can hold more than 101,000 people!

Fort Recovery

★ **Fort Recovery:** That is the name of the town and of a fort built by General Anthony Wayne in the 1790s. Today, you can see what the walls and the blockhouse looked like at this reconstruction of the wooden fort.

Harrison

★ **American Watchmakers- Clockmakers Institute Museum:** Learn all about clocks, watches, and other timepieces at this museum. The displays have everything from ancient sundials to a 28-foot (8.5 m) swinging pendulum.

MINI-BIO

GEORGE WASHINGTON WILLIAMS: OHIO LEGISLATOR

George Washington Williams (1849–1891) was the first African American to serve in the Ohio house of representatives. He had been a soldier in the Civil War and then became a minister and a lawyer. He wrote a history of African Americans and of African American troops in the Civil War. He also investigated human rights abuses in the Congo area of Africa, then owned by King Leopold of Belgium.

❓ **Want to know more?** See www.georgewashingtonwilliams.org/legislators.cfm?letter=W&legislator=89

Lebanon

★ **Fort Ancient State Memorial:** See 18,000 feet (5,500 m) of Native American earthworks built about 2,000 years ago. In the museum at Fort Ancient, exhibits tell the story of Ohio's Native peoples, dating back 15,000 years.

SOUTH-EASTERN

THINGS TO DO: Tour a mansion, climb up a gorge, or learn about the history of the National Road.

Chillicothe

★ **Adena Mansion & Gardens:** Beauty and history meet at Adena, the estate of Thomas Worthington, one of Ohio's first U.S. senators. The view across the Scioto River is so spectacular that it is on the Great Seal of the State of Ohio.

Lancaster

★ **Sherman House Museum:** A little brown house honors the memory of Civil War general William T. Sherman and his brother Senator John Sherman, who fought for fair business practices. The Sherman Antitrust Act was named for John.

Marietta

★ **Campus Martius Museum:** This museum is a monument to migration, including the movements of Native Americans and of people from rural areas to the cities. The rustic home of Rufus Putnam, founder of Marietta, is enclosed inside the museum.

Zanesville

★ **National Road/Zane Grey Museum:** A 136-foot (41 m) diorama at this museum tells the story of the National Road. Begun in 1806, it stretched from Maryland to Illinois. Another display is devoted to Western novelist Zane Grey.

Logan

★ **Hocking Hills State Park:** Do you like waterfalls, steep cliffs, and gorgeous gorges? You can see all of this along the 26 miles (42 km) of scenic hiking trails in this rugged area.

Hocking Hills State Park

SCIENCE, TECHNOLOGY, & MATH PROJECTS

Make weather maps, graph population statistics, and research endangered species that live in the state.

120

PRIMARY VS. SECONDARY SOURCES

121

So what are primary and secondary sources? And what's the diff? This section explains all that and where you can find them.

BIOGRAPHICAL DICTIONARY

133

This at-a-glance guide highlights some of the state's most important and influential people. Visit this section and read about their contributions to the state, the country, and the world.

RESOURCES

Books, Web sites, DVDs, and more. Take a look at these additional sources for information about the state.

137

WRITING PROJECTS

★ ★ ★

Write a Memoir, Journal, or Editorial for Your School Newspaper!

Picture Yourself . . .

★ On a fur-trading trip with your father. Describe your trip down the rivers of Ohio. Explain what kind of boat you travel in and what you brought with you to trade. Who would you be trading with? Where would you be going? What would your responsibilities be?

   SEE: Chapter 3, pages 35–36.

   GO TO: www.ohiohistorycentral.org/entry. php?rec=1555

★ Living in the Fort Ancient village and watching a chunkey game. Imagine you're covering the game for your school newspaper. What would the atmosphere of the sport be like? Who would you be rooting for? What would happen?

   SEE: Chapter 2, pages 27–31.

   GO TO: www.nku.edu/~anthro/ nkuanthromuseum/FAweb/AFortAncientVillage. htm

★ Helping people escape slavery on the Underground Railroad. Talk about the reasons your family decided to get involved. Did they have any doubts? Discuss how people fleeing slavery locate your house. Where do you hide them? How do you help them find the next stop on the Underground Railroad?

   SEE: Chapter 4, pages 49–52.

   GO TO: www.nationalgeographic.com/ railroad/

Create an Election Brochure or Web Site!

Run for office! Throughout this book, you've read about some issues that concern Ohio today. As a candidate for governor of Ohio, create a campaign brochure or Web site.

★ Explain how you meet the qualifications to be governor of Ohio.

★ Talk about the three or four major issues you'll focus on if you're elected.

★ Remember, you'll be responsible for Ohio's budget. How would you spend the taxpayers' money?

   SEE: Chapter Seven, pages 88–90.

   GO TO: Ohio's government Web site at www. ohio.gov.

Create an interview script with a person from Ohio!

★ Research various Ohioans, such as Neil Armstrong, Gloria Steinem, Drew Carey, Larry Doby, Rita Dove, or Thomas Edison.

★ Based on your research, pick one person you would most like to talk with.

★ Write a script of the interview. What questions would you ask? How would this person answer? Create a question-and-answer format. You can supplement this writing project with a voice-recording dramatization of the interview.

   SEE: Chapters Five, Six, and Seven, pages 58–95, and the Biographical Dictionary, pages 133–136.

   GO TO: www.ohiohistorycentral.org/ subcategory.php?c=H&s=PEO

ART PROJECTS

★ ★ ★

Create a PowerPoint Presentation or Visitors' Guide

Welcome to Ohio!

Ohio is a great place to visit and to live! From its natural beauty to its bustling cities and historical sites, there's plenty to see and do. In your PowerPoint presentation or brochure, highlight 10 to 15 of Ohio's amazing landmarks. Be sure to include:

★ a map of the state showing where these sites are located

★ photos, illustrations, Web links, natural history facts, geographic stats, climate and weather info, and descriptions of plants and wildlife

SEE: Chapter One, pages 8–21, and Chapter Nine, pages 108–115.

GO TO: The official tourism Web site for Ohio at www.discoverohio.com. Download and print maps, photos, and vacationing ideas for tourists.

Illustrate the Lyrics to the Ohio State Song ("Beautiful Ohio")

Use markers, paints, photos, collages, colored pencils, or computer graphics to illustrate the lyrics to "Beautiful Ohio." Turn your illustrations into a picture book, or scan them into PowerPoint and add music.

SEE: The lyrics to "Beautiful Ohio" on page 128.

GO TO: The Ohio state government Web site at www.ohio.gov to find out more about the origin of the state song.

Research Ohio's State Quarter

From 1999 to 2008, the U.S. Mint introduced new quarters commemorating each of the 50 states in the order that they were admitted to the Union. Each state's quarter features a unique design on its back, or reverse.

GO TO: www.usmint.gov/kids and find out what's featured on the back of the Ohio quarter.

★ Research the significance of the image. Who designed the quarter? Who chose the final design?

★ Design your own Ohio quarter. What images would you choose for the reverse?

★ Make a poster showing the Ohio quarter and label each image.

SCIENCE, TECHNOLOGY, & MATH PROJECTS

★ ★ ★

Graph Population Statistics!

★ Compare population statistics (such as ethnic background, birth, death, and literacy rates) in Ohio counties or major cities.

★ In your graph or chart, look at population density and write sentences describing what the population statistics show; graph one set of population statistics and write a paragraph explaining what the graphs reveal.

SEE: Chapter Six, pages 72–75.

GO TO: The official Web site for the U.S. Census Bureau at www.census.gov and at http://quickfacts.census.gov/qfd/states/39000.html, to find out more about population statistics, how they work, and what the statistics are for Ohio.

Create a Weather Map of Ohio!

Use your knowledge of Ohio's geography to research and identify conditions that result in specific weather events. What is it about the geography of Ohio that makes it vulnerable to things such as tornadoes? Create a weather map or poster that shows the weather patterns over the state. Include a caption explaining the technology used to measure weather phenomena such as tornadoes, and provide data.

SEE: Chapter One, pages 16–17.

GO TO: The National Oceanic and Atmospheric Administration's National Weather Service Web site at www.weather.gov for weather maps and forecasts for Ohio.

Track Endangered Species

Using your knowledge of Ohio's wildlife, research which animals and plants are endangered or threatened.

★ Find out what the state is doing to protect these species.

★ Chart known populations of the animals and plants, and report on changes in certain geographic areas.

SEE: Chapter One, page 20.

GO TO: Web sites such as www.dnr.state.oh.us/tabid/6005/default.aspx for lists of endangered species in Ohio.

Snowshoe hare

PRIMARY VS. SECONDARY SOURCES

★ ★ ★

What's the Diff?

Your teacher may require at least one or two primary sources and one or two secondary sources for your assignment. So, what's the difference between the two?

★ **Primary sources are original.** You are reading the actual words of someone's diary, journal, letter, autobiography, or interview. Primary sources can also be photographs, maps, prints, cartoons, news/film footage, posters, first-person newspaper articles, drawings, musical scores, and recordings. By the way, when you conduct a survey, interview someone, shoot a video, or take photographs to include in a project, you are creating primary sources!

★ **Secondary sources are what you find in encyclopedias, textbooks, articles, biographies, and almanacs.** These are written by a person or group of people who tell about something that happened to someone else. Secondary sources also recount what another person said or did. This book is an example of a secondary source.

Now that you know what primary sources are—where can you find them?

★ **Your school or local library:** Check the library catalog for collections of original writings, government documents, musical scores, and so on. Some of this material may be stored on microfilm. The Library of Congress Web site (www.loc.gov) is an excellent online resource for primary source materials.

★ **Historical societies:** These organizations keep historical documents, photographs, and other materials. Staff members can help you find what you are looking for. History museums are also great places to see primary sources firsthand.

★ **The Internet:** There are lots of sites that have primary sources you can download and use in a project or assignment.

TIMELINE

★ ★ ★

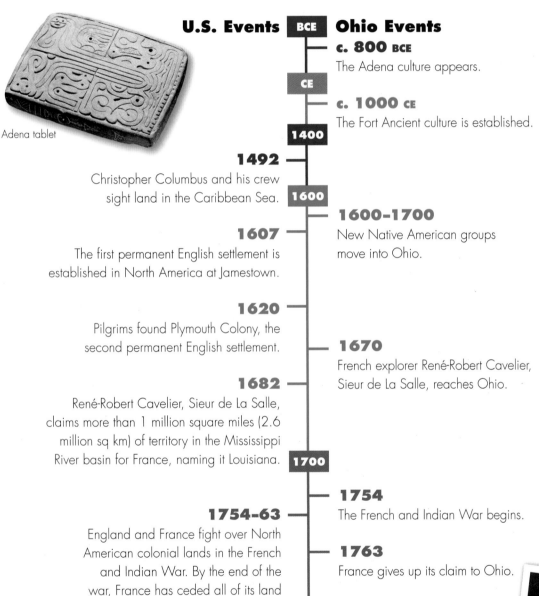

Adena tablet

U.S. Events	BCE	Ohio Events

BCE

CE

c. 800 BCE
The Adena culture appears.

c. 1000 CE
The Fort Ancient culture is established.

1400

1492
Christopher Columbus and his crew sight land in the Caribbean Sea.

1600

1600–1700
New Native American groups move into Ohio.

1607
The first permanent English settlement is established in North America at Jamestown.

1620
Pilgrims found Plymouth Colony, the second permanent English settlement.

1670
French explorer René-Robert Cavelier, Sieur de La Salle, reaches Ohio.

1682
René-Robert Cavelier, Sieur de La Salle, claims more than 1 million square miles (2.6 million sq km) of territory in the Mississippi River basin for France, naming it Louisiana.

1700

1754
The French and Indian War begins.

1754–63
England and France fight over North American colonial lands in the French and Indian War. By the end of the war, France has ceded all of its land west of the Mississippi to Spain and its Canadian territories to England.

1763
France gives up its claim to Ohio.

1763–64
Pontiac leads Native Americans in a rebellion.

1776
Thirteen American colonies declare their independence from Britain.

Pontiac

U.S. Events

Ohio Events

1787
The U.S. Constitution is written.

Marietta

1788
Marietta, Ohio's first permanent white settlement, is founded.

1794
Native Americans are defeated in the Battle of Fallen Timbers.

1800

1803
The Louisiana Purchase almost doubles the size of the United States.

1803
Ohio becomes a state.

1812–15
The United States and Great Britain fight the War of 1812.

1812
Columbus becomes the capital.

1830
The Indian Removal Act forces eastern Native American groups to relocate west of the Mississippi River.

1830-1860
At least 40,000 people escape slavery on the Underground Railroad through Ohio.

1833
The Ohio and Erie Canal is completed.

1846–48
The United States fights a war with Mexico over western territories in the Mexican War.

1861–65
The American Civil War is fought between the Northern Union and the Southern Confederacy; it ends with the surrender of the Confederate army, led by General Robert E. Lee.

Underground Railroad passage at Steubenville

1863
President Abraham Lincoln frees all slaves in the Southern Confederacy with the Emancipation Proclamation.

1871
B. F. Goodrich becomes the first rubber company in Akron.

1898
The United Mine Workers wins an eight-hour workday.

U.S. Events `1900` **Ohio Events**

1917–18
The United States engages in World War I.

1929
The stock market crashes, plunging the United States more deeply into the Great Depression.

1930
Cleveland's African American population rises to 72,000.

1937
Rubber workers in Akron successfully stage a strike.

1941–45
The United States engages in World War II.

1951–53
The United States engages in the Korean War.

1959
The St. Lawrence Seaway opens.

1960s
Civil rights protests are held across Ohio.

1964–73
The United States engages in the Vietnam War.

1967
Cleveland elects Carl Burton Stokes the first African American mayor of a major U.S. city.

1970s
Many of Ohio's big steel mills shut down.

1991
The United States and other nations engage in the brief Persian Gulf War against Iraq.

`2000`

2001
Terrorists hijack four U.S. aircraft and crash them into the World Trade Center in New York City, the Pentagon in Arlington, Virginia, and a Pennsylvania field, killing thousands.

2001
A new Jeep plant opens in Toledo.

Jeep assembly in Toledo

2003
The United States and coalition forces invade Iraq.

GLOSSARY

★ ★ ★

abolitionists people who were opposed to slavery and worked to end it

allies nations that are on the same side in a conflict

archaeologists people who study the remains of past human societies

carbon a chemical element found in all living things and things that were once alive

civil rights basic human rights that all citizens in a society are entitled to, such as the right to vote

colony a community settled in a new land but with ties to another government

confederation an association of groups that come together with common goals

discrimination unequal treatment based on race, gender, religion, or other factors

earthworks works of art made from piled-up soil

ghettos slum areas of cities occupied by disadvantaged people

interurbans small trains or trolley cars connecting two or more cities

juvenile referring to young people

lynching to kill by mob without a lawful trial

metropolitan areas cities and all the suburbs surrounding them

missionaries people who try to convert others to a religion

sediment material eroded from rocks and deposited elsewhere by wind, water, or glaciers

speculators people who buy land or other items and hope to sell for more than they paid

sponsor to propose or write a bill

stocks shares in the ownership of a company

strike an organized refusal to work, usually as a sign of protest about working conditions

suffragettes women in the early 1900s who worked for women's right to vote

transmissions mechanisms for transmitting power from a motor vehicle's engine to its wheels

tyranny a cruel and unfair use of power

union an organization formed by workers to try to improve working conditions and wages

veto to reject a proposed law

FAST FACTS

★ ★ ★

State Symbols

State seal

Statehood date	March 1,1803, the 17th state
Origin of state name	Iroquois word for "great river"
State capital	Columbus
State nickname	Buckeye State
State motto	"With God, all things are possible"
State animal	White-tailed deer
State beverage	Tomato juice
State bird	Cardinal
State flower	Scarlet carnation
State wildflower	White trillium
State fish	Walleye
State insect	Ladybug
State reptile	Black racer snake
State invertebrate fossil	Isotelus (trilobite)
State gem	Ohio flint
State song	"Beautiful Ohio" (See page 128 for lyrics.)
State tree	Buckeye
State fair	Mid-August at Columbus

Geography

Total area; rank	44,825 square miles (116,096 sq km); 34th
Land; rank	40,948 square miles (106,055 sq km); 35th
Water; rank	3,877 square miles (10,041 sq km); 14th
Inland water; rank	378 square miles (979 sq km); 37th
Great Lakes; rank	3,499 square miles (9,062 sq km); 4th
Geographic center	Delaware County, 25 miles (40 km) north-northeast of Columbus
Latitude	38° 27' N to 41° 58' N
Longitude	80° 32' W to 84° 49' W
Highest point	Campbell Hill, 1,550 feet (472 m), located in Logan County
Lowest point	Ohio River, 455 feet (139 m), located in Hamilton County

Largest city Columbus
Longest river Ohio River, 451 miles (726 km)
Number of counties 88

Population

Population; rank (2006 estimate) 11,478,006; 7th
Density (2006 estimate) 280 persons per square mile (108 per sq km)
Population distribution (2000 census) 77% urban, 23% rural
Race (2005 estimate) White persons: 85.1%*

Black persons: 11.9%*
Asian persons: 1.4%*
American Indian and Alaska Native persons: 0.2%*
Native Hawaiian and Other Pacific Islander: 0.0%*
Persons reporting two or more races: 1.3%
Persons of Hispanic or Latino origin: 2.3%†
White persons not Hispanic: 83.1%

Includes persons reporting only one race.
†Hispanics may be of any race, so they are also included in applicable race categories.

Weather

Record high temperature 113°F (45°C) near Gallipolis on July 21, 1934
Record low temperature −39°F (−39°C) at Milligan on February 10, 1899
Average July temperature 75°F (24°C)
Average January temperature 28°F (−2°C)
Average annual precipitation 38 inches (97 cm)

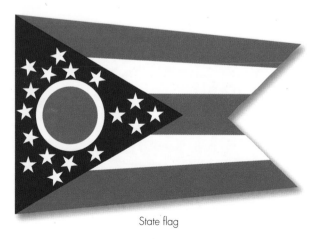

State flag

STATE SONG

"Beautiful Ohio"
Music by Mary Earl, words by Ballard MacDonald

In 1969, the Ohio legislature adopted "Beautiful Ohio" as Ohio's state song. Mary Earl composed the music, and Ballard MacDonald wrote the original lyrics. In 1989, with the permission of the Ohio legislature, Wilbert B. McBride altered the lyrics.

I sailed away;
Wandered afar;
Crossed the mighty restless sea;
Looked for where I ought to be.
Cities so grand, mountains above,
Led to this land I love.

Chorus:
Beautiful Ohio, where the golden grain
Dwarf the lovely flowers in the summer rain.
Cities rising high, silhouette the sky.
Freedom is supreme in this majestic land;
Mighty factories seem to hum in tune, so grand.
Beautiful Ohio, thy wonders are in view,
Land where my dreams all come true!

NATURAL AREAS AND HISTORIC SITES

National Park

Ohio's *Cuyahoga Valley National Park* consists of 33,000 acres (13,355 ha) of diverse habitat for wildlife and stands as Ohio's only national park.

National Memorials

The *David Berger National Memorial* honors David Berger and the other 10 Israeli athletes who were assassinated by Palestinian terrorists during the 1972 Olympic Games in Munich, Germany.

Perry's Victory and International Peace Memorial commemorates Commodore Oliver Perry's victory at the Battle of Lake Erie.

National Historical Parks

The *Dayton Aviation Heritage National Historical Park* honors the Wright brothers and their friend, poet Paul Laurence Dunbar, for their cultural and historical contributions.

Hopewell Culture National Historical Park features earthen mounds built by the Hopewell people.

National Historic Sites

The *First Ladies National Historic Site* honors and preserves the contributions of America's first ladies.

The *James A. Garfield National Historic Site* and the *William Howard Taft National Historic Site* preserve the homes and the surrounding lands of Garfield, the 20th U.S. president, and Taft, the 27th U.S. president.

National Forest

Located in the rugged Appalachian foothills, *Wayne National Forest* covers about 250,000 acres (101,000 ha). The welcome center at Athens is a good place to begin a visit. Displays tell about geology and wildlife of the forest.

State Parks and Forests

Ohio has 74 state parks that offer a variety of outdoor activities, beautiful scenery, and history, including *Indian Lake State Park*, *Marblehead Lighthouse State Park*, *Wolf Run State Park*, and *Great Seal State Park*.

SPORTS TEAMS

★ ★ ★

NCAA Teams (Division I)

Bowling Green State University *Falcons*
Cleveland State University *Vikings*
Kent State University *Golden Flashes*
Miami University *Redskins*
Ohio State University *Buckeyes*
Ohio University *Bobcats*
University of Akron *Zips*
University of Cincinnati *Bearcats*
University of Dayton *Flyers*
University of Toledo *Rockets*
Wright State University *Raiders*
Xavier University *Musketeers*

PROFESSIONAL SPORTS TEAMS

★ ★ ★

Major League Baseball
Cincinnati *Reds*
Cleveland *Indians*

National Football League
Cincinnati *Bengals*
Cleveland *Browns*

National Basketball Association
Cleveland *Cavaliers*

National Hockey League
Columbus *Blue Jackets*

Major League Soccer
Columbus *Crew*

CULTURAL INSTITUTIONS

Libraries

The *Archives/Library of the Ohio Historical Society* (Columbus) collects, preserves, and makes available to the public information concerning Ohio's history.

Cincinnati Historical Society, Martha Kinney Cooper Ohioana Library (Columbus), and the *Archive of Ohio Folklore* (Miami University) all have fine collections on Ohio history.

The Rutherford B. Hayes Presidential Center (Fremont) is located at the president's Spiegel Grove estate. The library houses Hayes's papers and books on 19th-century American life. The museum displays exhibits on the life and times of Hayes and his family.

Museums

The *Cincinnati Art Museum* (Cincinnati) contains collections of paintings, sculptures, and other artwork from around the world.

The *Cleveland Museum of Art* (Cleveland) has a permanent collection that includes more than 40,000 objects.

The *Dayton Art Institute* (Dayton) has collections of African, American, European, and Oceanic art.

The *Ohio Historical Center* (Columbus) has collections and exhibits devoted to Ohio's archaeology, history, and wildlife.

Taft Museum of Art (Cincinnati) includes collections ranging from European masterworks and 19th-century American paintings to Chinese ceramics and works of art.

Performing Arts

Ohio has six major opera companies, six major symphony orchestras, and seven major dance companies.

Universities and Colleges

In 2006, Ohio had 59 public and 64 private institutions of higher learning.

ANNUAL EVENTS

January–March

Ohio Winter Ski Carnival in Mansfield (February)

American-Canadian Sport Show in Cleveland (March)

Buzzard Day in Hinckley (March)

Maple Syrup Festival near Oxford (March)

April–June

Geauga County Maple Festival in Chardon (April)

James Wright Poetry Festival in Martins Ferry (April)

Appalachian Festival in Cincinnati (May)

Walleye Festival in Port Clinton (May)

Cherry Festival in Bellevue (June)

Festival of the Fish in Vermilion (June)

Memorial Golf Tournament in Dublin (June)

Ports and Maritime Festival in Cleveland (June)

Roy Rogers Festival in Portsmouth (June)

July–September

Dayton Air Show in Vandalia (July)

Jamboree in the Hills in Morristown (July)

Pro Football Hall of Fame Festival in Canton (July)

Ohio State Fair in Columbus (August)

Salt Fork Arts & Crafts Festival in Cambridge (August)

Appalachia Heritage Fest in New Lexington (September)

Grape Jamboree in Geneva (September)

Ohio River Sternwheel Festival in Marietta (September)

Riverfest in Cincinnati (September)

Tomato Festival in Reynoldsburg (September)

October–December

Apple Butter Stirrin' in Coshocton (October)

Bob Evans Farm Festival in Rio Grande (October)

The Hayes Civil War Encampment & Reenactment in Fremont (October)

Johnny Appleseed Festival in Brunswick (October)

Paul Bunyan Show in Nelsonville (October)

Pumpkin Show in Circleville (October)

Christmas at Ohio Village in Columbus (December)

Christmas Candlelightings in Coshocton (December)

Winterfest at Kings Island near Cincinnati (December)

BIOGRAPHICAL DICTIONARY

Sherwood Anderson (1876–1941) was a short-story writer and novelist born in Camden. His 1919 novel, *Winesburg, Ohio,* was based on his experiences growing up in Clyde.

Neil Armstrong (1930–), a native of Wapakoneta, was the first person to walk on the moon. After setting foot on it, he said, "That's one small step for man, one giant leap for mankind." He later became a government adviser, university professor, and businessman.

Ohio Columbus Barber (1841–1920) founded a company that became the Diamond Match Company of Akron. In the early 1900s, his company learned to make phosphorus-free matches, which were safer for the workers.

Kathleen Battle (1948–) is an opera star who has made many recordings and sung in television concerts and on movie sound tracks, such as *Fantasia 2000*. She was born in Portsmouth.

Daniel Carter Beard (1850–1941) was a magazine illustrator who formed youth groups related to the magazines. One of his groups, Boy Pioneers, became the Boy Scouts of America. He also helped his sister found the Camp Fire Girls. He was born in Cincinnati.

George Bellows (1882–1925) painted realistic scenes of city life, including street children. He was born in Columbus.

Kathleen Battle

Blue Jacket, or Weyapiersenwah (1740s?–1810?), was a Shawnee leader who fought to keep European settlers out of Ohio. He fought at the Battle of Fallen Timbers and signed the Treaty of Greenville.

Frances Payne Bolton (1885–1977) was the first Ohio woman elected to the U.S. House of Representatives. She served 14 terms and worked to improve education and public health.

Erma Bombeck (1927–1996), a native of Dayton, wrote a funny newspaper column and 15 best-selling humor books about her life as a mother and homemaker.

Hallie Q. Brown See page 53.

John Brown (1800–1859), who grew up in Hudson, dedicated his life to fighting slavery and slaveholders. He was arrested during a raid on a U.S. arsenal in Harpers Ferry, Virginia (now West Virginia). When the state hanged him for treason, his name became a rallying cry for abolitionists nationwide.

Drew Carey (1958–) is a comedian and game show host whose hit TV show, *The Drew Carey Show*, was set in his native Cleveland.

Joseph F. Carr (1880–1939) of Columbus was a newspaper reporter who helped establish the National Football League and served as its president from 1922 to 1939.

Neil Armstrong

Anthony Joseph Celebrezze Sr. (1910–1998) was a mayor of Cleveland who helped create Medicare in the 1960s as secretary of the U.S. Department of Health, Education, and Welfare.

Salmon P. Chase See page 92.

Peter H. Clark (1829–1925), a native of Cincinnati, published *The Herald of Freedom*, the Midwest's first African American newspaper.

Arthur Holly Compton (1892–1962) won the 1927 Nobel Prize in Physics for his work with X rays and cosmic rays. He also helped develop the atomic bomb. He was born in Wooster.

George Armstrong Custer (1839–1876), a native of New Rumley, was a U.S. cavalry leader. He fought in the Civil War and against Native Americans in the West.

Dorothy Dandridge (1923–1965) was a singer and the first black actress nominated for an Academy Award. She was from Cleveland.

Clarence Darrow (1857–1938) was a lawyer who took on controversial cases. He defended labor leaders and people accused of crimes that carried the death penalty. He defended John Scopes for teaching evolution in Tennessee schools in the historic "Monkey Trial." He grew up in Farmington.

Dorothy Dandridge

Doris Day (1924–) is the stage name of Academy Award–winning actor and singer Doris Mary Ann von Kappelhoff. She starred in classic movies such as *The Pajama Game* (1957) and *Please Don't Eat the Daisies* (1960). She was born in Cincinnati.

Phyllis Diller (1917–) is a comedian, actor, author, and concert pianist who grew up in Lima. She is also known for her work with cancer charities.

Larry Doby See page 80.

Rita Dove (1952–), a native of Akron, is a Pulitzer Prize–winning poet and teacher. In 1993, she became the country's youngest and first African American poet laureate.

Paul Laurence Dunbar (1872–1906), a poet, novelist, and short-story writer, was married to poet Alice Dunbar-Nelson, and he was a great friend of the Wright brothers.

Sarah Jane Woodson Early (1825–1907) was an educator from Chillicothe and an African American leader in the Women's Christian Temperance Union, a national organization that worked to ban alcohol.

Thomas Alva Edison (1847–1931) was an inventor who had patents on more than 1,000 inventions, including an incandescent lightbulb, the phonograph, and a motion picture camera. He was born in Milan.

M. Siobhan Fennessy See page 21.

Harvey Samuel Firestone (1868–1938) founded Akron's Firestone Tire and Rubber Company.

Clark Gable (1901–1960), a native of Cadiz, was an Academy Award–winning actor whose movies included *It Happened One Night* (1934) and *Gone with the Wind* (1939).

James A. Garfield See page 95.

John Glenn Jr. (1921–) was one of the first seven original U.S. astronauts. In 1962, he became the first American to orbit Earth. He served as a U.S. senator from Ohio from 1974 to 1999. In 1998, he was aboard the space shuttle *Discovery*, becoming the oldest person to travel in space.

Benjamin Franklin Goodrich (1841–1888) moved his rubber company from New York to Akron. The B. F. Goodrich Company was the first rubber company in Akron and helped make it the "rubber capital of the world."

Ulysses S. Grant See page 95.

Elisha Gray (1835–1901) of Barnesville claimed to have invented the telephone before Alexander Graham Bell. Gray lost the patent fight, but founded the Western Electric Manufacturing Company in 1872.

Zane Grey (1872–1939) was a popular author of Western short stories and novels, including *Riders of the Purple Sage* and *The Thundering Herd*. He was from Zanesville, a city founded by his ancestors.

Arsenio Hall (1955–) is a comedian, talk-show host, and actor from Cleveland.

Warren G. Harding See page 95.

Benjamin Harrison See page 95.

William Henry Harrison See page 95.

Rutherford B. Hayes See page 95.

Arsenio Hall

John Heisman (1869–1936) coached several football teams, including the Oberlin College team. The Heisman Memorial Trophy is named in his honor.

Bob Hope (1903–2003) was a comedian and movie star. He grew up in Cleveland and got his start in show business there.

Charles F. Kettering See page 102.

Little Turtle See page 41.

Barbara Alice Mann See page 31.

Dean Martin (1917–1995) was a popular singer and movie and TV star. He was born in Steubenville.

William McKinley See page 95.

Betty D. Montgomery (1948–) became Ohio's first woman attorney general in 1990.

Garrett Augustus Morgan (1877–1963) invented sewing equipment and devices to improve traffic safety, including a kind of traffic signal. He lived in Cleveland.

Toni Morrison See page 77.

Paul Newman (1925–) is an actor, director, and cofounder of Newman's Own food products. He was born in Shaker Heights.

Jack Nicklaus (1940–), a native of Columbus, is a golfer who won four U.S. Opens, three British Opens, five PGA championships, and six Masters titles before retiring in 2005.

Annie Oakley (1860–1926) was a sharpshooter who appeared in "Buffalo Bill" Cody's Wild West Show. She was born near North Star, in western Ohio.

John Glenn Jr.

Jesse Owens (1913–1980) was one of the greatest track-and-field athletes ever. He won four gold medals at the 1936 Olympics, and in 1976 he was awarded the Medal of Freedom. He grew up in Cleveland.

Leroy "Satchel" Paige (1906–1982) was a pitcher who became the first African American in Major League Baseball when the Cleveland Indians hired him in 1946.

Pontiac See page 37.

John Rankin (1793–1886) was born in Tennessee, but moved to Ripley in 1822. He became one of Ohio's first and most active conductors on the Underground Railroad.

Judith Resnik (1949–1986) was an electrical engineer and astronaut from Akron. She was among the crew on the *Challenger* space shuttle that exploded in 1986.

Charles Francis Richter (1900–1985) invented the Richter Scale for measuring the power of earthquakes. He was born in Hamilton.

Roy Rogers See page 78.

Albert Sabin (1906–1993) developed a vaccine against polio at the Cincinnati Children's Hospital.

Frank Seiberling (1859–1955) founded the Goodyear Tire & Rubber Company in Akron.

Martin Sheen See page 79.

William Tecumseh Sherman (1820–1891) was a Union army general from Lancaster who played a major role during the Civil War.

Judith Resnik

Joe Shuster (1914–1992) and his Cleveland neighbor **Jerry Siegel (1914–1996)** created the comic book hero Superman.

Harry C. Smith See page 62.

Steven Spielberg (1946–) is an Academy Award–winning director. He was born in Cincinnati.

Steven Spielberg

Gloria Steinem See page 68.

Robert Lawrence Stine (1943–) is the author of the popular and scary Goosebumps series of children's books. He is from Columbus.

Carl Burton Stokes See page 67.

Louis Stokes See page 90.

Harriet Beecher Stowe See page 50.

William Howard Taft See page 95.

James Grover Thurber (1894–1961), a native of Columbus, was a cartoonist and author of funny stories.

George Washington Williams See page 114.

Victoria Claflin Woodhull See page 94.

Granville T. Woods See page 100.

Orville Wright (1871–1948) and **Wilbur Wright (1867–1912)** were bicycle shop owners in Dayton who built the first successful airplane in 1903.

David Zeisberger (1721–1808) was a missionary who tried to convert the Delaware people to Christianity.

RESOURCES

BOOKS

Nonfiction

Arthur, Joe, and R. L. Stine. *It Came from Ohio: My Life As a Writer*. New York: Scholastic, 1997.

Barker, Charles Ferguson. *Under Ohio: The Story of Ohio's Rocks and Fossils*. Athens: Ohio University Press, 2007.

Coleman, Loren, Andy Henderson, and James A. Willis. *Weird Ohio*. New York: Sterling, 2006.

Doherty, Kieran. *William Howard Taft: America's 27th President*. Danbury, Conn.: Children's Press, 2004.

Edge, Laura Bufano. *William McKinley*. Minneapolis: Lerner, 2007.

Jackson, Tom. *The Ohio River*. Milwaukee: Gareth Stevens, 2003.

Rice, Earle. *Ulysses S. Grant: Defender of the Union*. Greensboro, N.C.: Morgan Reynolds, 2005.

Schonberg, Marcia. *Ohio Native Peoples*. Chicago: Heinemann, 2003.

Schonberg, Marcia. *Ohio Plants and Animals*. Chicago: Heinemann, 2003.

Fiction

Aller, Susan Bivin. *Living with the Senecas: A Story About Mary Jemison*. Minneapolis: Lerner, 2007.

Anderson, Sherwood. *Winesburg, Ohio*. New York: Bantam Classics, 1995.

Mackall, Dandi Daley. *The Legend of Ohio*. Chelsea, Mich.: Sleeping Bear Press, 2005.

Mackall, Dandi Daley. *Wild Thing* (Winnie the Horse Gentler, Book 1). Carol Stream, Ill.: Tyndale Kids, 2007.

Pearsall, Shelley. *Crooked River*. New York: Yearling, 2007.

Raven, Margot Theis. *Night Boat to Freedom*. New York: Farrar, Straus and Giroux, 2006.

Willis, Patricia. *Danger Along the Ohio*. New York: HarperTrophy, 1999.

Zinnen, Linda. *The Dragons of Spratt, Ohio*. New York: HarperCollins, 2004.

DVDs

American Experience — Ulysses S. Grant, Warrior President. PBS Paramount, 2005.
Discoveries America — Ohio. Bennett-Watt Entertainment, 2004.
Historic Travel US — Ohio Surges On. Tapeworm Video, 2005.
Ohio State — The History of Buckeye Football. Warner Home Video, 2005.
The Prize Winner of Defiance, Ohio. DreamWorks Video, 2006.
Rivers of North America: Ohio River. Film Ideas, Inc., 2006.
Swing State Ohio. JLP Media, 2007.

WEB SITES AND ORGANIZATIONS

City of Columbus: Official Web Site
www.columbus.gov/where/fun.asp
For dozens of fun facts about Ohio.

Discover Ohio
http://consumer.discoverohio.com/
Find out where to go and what to see and do in Ohio.

Ohio Historical Society
www.ohiohistory.org/
For a wealth of primary source documents relating to Ohio history.

Ohio History Central
www.ohiohistorycentral.org/
Browse a wealth of articles related to Ohio history, geography, events, and people.

Ohio Kids
www.ohiokids.org/ohjonesintro/
To find out about places to visit and activities just for kids.

Ohio Memory Project
www.ohiomemory.org/
For an online scrapbook of primary source images relating to all aspects of Ohio and its history.

Ohio Public Library Information Network: Discover Ohio
www.oplin.lib.oh.us/main.php?Id=63&msg
Explore a variety of topics about Ohio, such as history, geography, and people, by following the links listed on this site.

Ohio's Prehistoric People
www.oplin.org/point/people/timeline.html
Find a timeline of the early settlement of Ohio by Native Americans.

State of Ohio
http://ohio.gov/
To learn about Ohio's government.

INDEX

★ ★ ★

AUTHOR'S TIPS AND SOURCE NOTES

★ ★ ★

In doing research on Ohio, I found myself getting lost in the many historical images available at the Ohio Memory Project's Online Scrapbook. The Ohio Historical Society has a wealth of newspaper articles, personal letters, pamphlets, and other materials for researchers. There is also an index of print and visual material available in libraries throughout Ohio.

The most delightful history book I found during my research was *Ohio: A History* by Walter Havighurst. It reads more like a novel than a history book and gives a feeling for the times, rather than just facts. Other books full of great information that I enjoyed included *Builders of Ohio, A Biographical History,* by Warren Van Tine and Michael D. Pierce, and *Best of the Best from Ohio Cookbook*.